TWENTIETH CENTURY INTERPRETATIONS
OF

MEASURE FOR MEASURE

A Collection of Critical Essays

Edited by

GEORGE L. GECKLE

Prentice-Hall, Inc.   A SPECTRUM BOOK   *Englewood Cliffs, N. J.*

Copyright © 1970 by Prentice Hall, Inc., Englewood Cliffs, New Jersey. A SPEC-
TRUM BOOK. All rights reserved. No part of this book may be reproduced in any
form or by any means without permission in writing from the publisher. P–13-
567719-X; C–13-567727-0. *Library of Congress Catalog Card Number 76–104844.*
Printed in the United States of America.

Current printing (last number):
10   9   8   7   6   5   4   3   2   1

PRENTICE-HALL INTERNATIONAL, INC. (*London*)
PRENTICE-HALL OF AUSTRALIA, PTY. LTD. (*Sydney*)
PRENTICE-HALL OF CANADA, LTD. (*Toronto*)
PRENTICE-HALL OF INDIA PRIVATE LIMITED (*New Delhi*)
PRENTICE-HALL OF JAPAN, INC. (*Tokyo*)

To Judy

Contents

Introduction

by George L. Geckle

I

We have little factual information about William Shakespeare's life. He was probably born on April 23, 1564, and records indicate that he was christened on April 26 of that year in Holy Trinity Church, Stratford on Avon. He died on April 23, 1616 and was buried in the church of his baptism.

Shakespeare was the third child of Mary Arden and John Shakespeare, a well-to-do tanner and glover of Stratford. He probably received a good grammar-school education in his native town. At the age of eighteen he married Anne Hathaway, his elder by eight years. They had three children, all christened in Holy Trinity Church in Stratford—Susanna on May 26, 1583, and the twins, Hamnet and Judith, on February 2, 1585.

Although nothing is actually known of Shakespeare's activities immediately before and after his marriage, he seems to have established himself in London as an actor and playwright by 1592. In 1599 his theatrical company, the Lord Chamberlain's Men (formed in 1594), built the Globe Theatre on the south side of the Thames. When James I ascended the throne in 1603, this company became the King's Men, and one of its first productions for the new sovereign was *Measure for Measure,* written in 1604 and performed at Whitehall on St. Stephen's Night (December 26) of that year.

As is the case with most of Shakespeare's work, little is known of the external circumstances surrounding the production of *Measure for Measure.* The play was never printed during his lifetime, and our only authoritative text is that in the First Folio of 1623. Moreover, apart from a reference in the *Revels Accounts* to the Whitehall performance on December 26, we have no record of its performance during the entire Jacobean period. Despite this, scholars have done much to provide us with an historical and critical context. For instance, in the first attempt to date the play, Edmond Malone noted that "from two passages in it, which seem intended as a courtly apology for the stately and ungracious demeanour of King James I.

on his entry into England, it appears probable that it was written not long after his accession [in 1603] to the throne." [1] The two passages, I. i. 67–72 and II. iv. 20–30, have since been cited both as indications of the play's date and as evidence that Shakespeare placed into the mouth of Duke Vincentio opinions that had earlier been expressed by James I in his book on the art of government, the *Basilicon Doron*, printed in 1599 and again published in March 1603.[2] If James's writings are indeed mirrored in the play, then not only is Shakespeare flattering his king but the case is perhaps strengthened for regarding the Duke as a guide to the play's meaning.

More important for a detailed understanding of *Measure for Measure* are G. B. Giraldi Cinthio's *Hecatommithi* (1565) and George Whetstone's ten-act play *Promos and Cassandra* (1578), on both of which Shakespeare drew. As Kenneth Muir points out,[3] a study of these sources makes it indubitably clear that Shakespeare's primary interest was "to write a play on the subject of forgiveness . . . Christian forgiveness—that is, the forgiveness of enemies." Since *Measure for Measure* treats this topic within the context of secular justice and the exercise of power, the title is replete with meaning, calling to mind both Old and New Testament allusions to a "measure" that is "measured" back to each one who "measures" it out.[4] Even external

---

[1] Edmond Malone, "An Attempt to Ascertain the Order in Which the Plays of Shakspeare Were Written" (1790), in *The Plays and Poems of William Shakspeare*, ed. Edmond Malone and James Boswell (London, 1821), II, 383.

[2] See the excerpt from J. W. Lever below.

[3] See the article by Muir below.

[4] See Exod. xxi:23–25: "23 But if death follow, then thou shalt pay life for life,/24 Eye for eye, tooth for tooth, hand for hand, foote for foote,/25 Burning for burning, wound for wound, stripe for stripe." Lev. xxiv:17–20: "17 He also that killeth any man, hee shalbe put to death./18 And he that killeth a beast, he shal restore it; beast for beast./19 Also if a man cause any blemish in his neighbour: as he hath done, so shall it be done to him:/20 Breach for breach, eie for eie, tooth for tooth: such a blemish as hee hath made in any, such shalbe repaied to him." Deut. xix:21: "Therefore thine eie shall have no compassion; but life for life, eie for eie, tooth for tooth, hand for hand, foote for foote." Matt. v:38–39: "38 Ye have heard that it hath bin said, An eye for an eye, and a tooth for a tooth:/39 But I say unto you, Resist not evill: but whosoever shall smite thee on the right cheeke, turne to him the other also." Matthew vii:1–2: "1 Judge not, that ye be not judged./2 For with what judgement ye judge, ye shall be judged, and with what measure ye mete, it shall be measured to you againe." Luke vi:35–38: "35 Therefore love ye your enemies, and do good, and lend, looking for nothing again, and your rewarde shalbe great, and yee shalbe the children of the most High: for he is kind unto the unkinde, and to the evill./36 Be ye therfore merciful, as your father also is merciful./37 Judge not, and ye shal not be judged: condemne not, and ye shal not be condemned: forgive, and ye shalbe forgiven./38 Give, and it shall be given unto you: a good measure, pressed down, shaken together and running over shal men give unto your bosome, for with what measure ye mete, with the same shal men mete to you againe."

evidence, in short, guides us quickly to the play's central issues, which are ethical in nature.

II

In the opening scene of *Measure for Measure* Duke Vincentio tells us that "Of government the properties to unfold/Would seem in me t'affect speech and discourse" (I. i. 3–4).[5] Nevertheless, in spite of his reticence, the major themes of the next five acts all relate in some way to "government." The Duke himself, for example, points out that Escalus is well versed in the "art and practice" (I. i. 12) of "common justice" (I. i. 11), thereby foreshadowing his good sense in the debate with Angelo and in his handling of Pompey and Elbow in Act II, scene i. Similarly, when the Duke calls Angelo forth and tells him that he, not Escalus, will rule and that "Mortality and mercy in Vienna/Live in thy tongue, and heart" (I. i. 44–45), he sets up for us a standard by which to judge the deputy's future acts. The Duke's allusions[6] to New Testament parables (lines 29–40) and his instructions to Angelo that "Your scope is as mine own,/So to enforce or qualify the laws/As to your soul seems good" (I. i. 64–66) further relate the exercise of power to the possibilities of human nature and the higher "government" of God.

In Act I, scene iii, the Duke's cryptic behavior is explained. There, about to disguise himself as a friar, the Duke makes four points that help to explain the motives and actions of several of the play's characters. First of all (lines 19–31), he notes that because the law has not been enforced Vienna is morally degenerate: "And Liberty plucks Justice by the nose,/The baby beats the nurse, and quite athwart/Goes all decorum" (I. iii. 29–31). Additional emblems of disorder have already been dramatized in the witty but vulgar conversation of Lucio and the two Gentlemen in Act I, scene ii, not to mention the obvious visual presence in that scene of Vienna's chief bawds, Mistress Overdone and Pompey. The Duke's next two points relate Vienna's depravity to his own failings as a ruler: "Sith 'twas my fault to give the people scope,/'Twould be my tyranny to strike and gall them" (I. iii. 35–36). Angelo, therefore, is to be a sort of scapegoat so that, as the Duke says, he himself will escape recriminations: "my nature never in the fight/To do in slander" (I. iii. 42–43). Ironically, he undergoes

---

(The above quotations are taken from the Geneva version of the Bible published in London in 1595. I have normalized "i/j" and "u/v."

[5] All quotations are from the Arden Shakespeare *Measure for Measure*, edited by J. W. Lever (London and Cambridge, Mass., 1965).

[6] See the article by G. Wilson Knight below.

a great amount of "slander," thanks to Lucio, "a kind of burr" (IV. iii. 177), who continually insults his disguised ruler and impugns his motives. The Duke's fourth and major point, however, relates directly to Angelo: "Lord Angelo is precise;/Stands at a guard with Envy; scarce confesses/That his blood flows; or that his appetite/Is more to bread than stone. Hence shall we see/If power change purpose, what our seemers be" (I. iii. 50–54). The chief action, in other words, is to be the test of Angelo as governor not only of Vienna but of himself.

To restore order, Angelo publishes at once a proclamation invoking the law against fornication, a law that has long been dormant.[7] Its first victims are Claudio and his pregnant fiancée Juliet. Part of their punishment is to be openly paraded through the streets on their way to prison, a punishment usually reserved for prostitutes. Ironically, certain genuine prostitutes will never be punished at all since, as Pompey tells us, "a wise burgher put in for them" (I. ii. 92).

The penalty to which Claudio is liable is death, but as if to extenuate his guilt Shakespeare allows him to make the point that "upon a true contract/I got possession of Julietta's bed" (I. ii. 134–35). The "true contract" is a betrothal contract, the technicalities of which in Renaissance times were extremely complex,[8] but it was probably sufficient for Shakespeare's audiences to know that betrothal contracts (*sponsalia per verba de praesenti*) were legally binding, even though the Church would not sanction the union until it had bestowed its formal blessing through marriage. Claudio and Juliet are, therefore, in Christian terms guilty of sin, and this explains Claudio's acknowledgment of guilt[9] when Lucio asks him why he is a prisoner. "From too much liberty, my Lucio. Liberty,/As surfeit, is the father of much fast;/So every scope by the immoderate use/Turns to restraint" (I. ii. 117–20). The terms "scope" and "liberty," recalling the Duke's speeches at I. i. 64–66 and I. iii. 29–31, expand into personal and private behavior the ethical relationships already indicated between justice, liberty, law enforcement, and self-discipline in the public domain.

Despite betrothal, Claudio is technically guilty of fornication under the old law revived by Angelo, and can be legally punished. We learn, however, that Mariana was once "affianced" (III. i. 213–23) to

---

[7] We read "nineteen zodiacs" at I.ii.157 and "fourteen years" at I.iii.21, but the discrepancy is unimportant in interpreting the play.

[8] See Davis P. Harding, "Elizabethan Betrothals and 'Measure for Measure,'" *Journal of English and Germanic Philology*, XLIV (1950), 139–58; Ernest Schanzer, "The Marriage-Contracts in *Measure for Measure*," *Shakespeare Survey*, XIII (1960), 81–89; S. Nagarajan, "*Measure for Measure* and Elizabethan Betrothals," *Shakespeare Quarterly*, XIV (1963), 115–19.

[9] Cf. Juliet's similar feelings in Act II, scene iii.

Angelo too, and in the Duke's words that he is Mariana's "husband on a pre-contract" (IV. i. 72),[10] as Claudio is Juliet's. Shakespeare obviously wants his audience to note the similarities between the two situations. Not only have both couples been betrothed but in both instances the wedding ceremony has not occurred because a dowry was not forthcoming (cf. I. ii. 138–42 and III. i. 221–22). Claudio, however, has kept his pledge to Juliet and wants to marry her. Angelo, who, as the Duke says, "scarce confesses/That his blood flows; or that his appetite/Is more to bread than stone," has jilted Mariana (see III. i. 222–30).

Angelo's "blood" [11] is the subject of conjecture by the libertine Lucio too. He tells Isabella that Angelo is "a man whose blood/Is very snow-broth; one who never feels/The wanton stings and motions of the sense" (I. iv. 57–59). This is also Angelo's own opinion, as is first made evident in his debate with Escalus at the beginning of Act II. Escalus argues that one should prune rather than indiscriminately chop down ("Let us be keen, and rather cut a little,/Than fall, and bruise to death." II. i. 5–6) and that Claudio's case should be handled in terms of its own peculiarities.[12] Angelo, on the other hand, stresses the strict letter of the law, an Old Testament "measure for measure." When Escalus asks Angelo to try to imagine himself in Claudio's place, Angelo argues: " 'Tis one thing to be tempted, Escalus,/Another thing to fall" (II. i. 17–18). Angelo, in fact, goes so far as to confuse justice with law: "What's open made to justice,/That justice seizes" (II. i. 21–22). Yet, as we have seen in Act I, scene ii, the relatively decent Claudio is to be punished for being caught, whereas the real bawds can escape because "a wise burgher put in for them." What happens when one simply equates law and justice is brought home to us in the unmitigated stupidity of the law's representative, Constable Elbow, who in his case against Pompey drives Escalus to ask: "Which is the wiser here, Justice or Iniquity?" (II. i. 169).

[10] Angelo and Mariana's betrothal has been called a *sponsalia per verba de futuro,* a promise to marry in the future; it was not legally binding until consummation occurred, hence the importance of the bed-trick that substitutes Mariana for Isabella.

[11] In Renaissance physiology "blood" was one of the four "humours" (the others being melancholy, phlegm, and choler) that combined to make up a man's temperament or "complexion." "Blood" was also thought to be the source of passion, especially sexual passion.

[12] Several critics have noted that *Measure for Measure,* and Escalus in particular, invokes the Aristotelian concept of equity (defined as "a correction of the law where it is defective owing to its universality"). See John W. Dickinson, "Renaissance Equity and *Measure for Measure," SQ,* XIII (1962), 287–97; Wilbur Dunkel, "Law and Equity in *Measure for Measure," SQ,* XIII (1962), 275–85; John Wasson, *"Measure for Measure*: A Play of Incontinence," *English Literary History,* XXVII (1960), 262–75.

The irony of Angelo's position is by now twofold: first, he never dreams that ultimately he too must face up to the concept of strict Old Testament justice that he invokes against Claudio; second, he knows himself so slightly that he remains oblivious to the possibility of his own temptation and fall. The temptation derives from the meeting between Angelo and Claudio's sister, Isabella, who has come to plead for him. She it is who first sets the divine standard of mercy against Angelo's law: "I do think that you might pardon him,/And neither heaven nor man grieve at the mercy" (II. ii. 49–50). Explicitly referring to Christ's sacrifice in her next lines (II. ii. 73–77), Isabella first invokes the Sermon on the Mount: "Judge not, that ye be not judged" (Matt. vii: 1) and then, with her reference to "man new made" (II. ii. 77–79), St. Paul's man newly made through Christ's mercy to all sinners (Col. iii: 9–10; Eph. iv: 20–24). Angelo's response is to confuse his own power to act with absolute justice: "Look, what I will not, that I cannot do" (II. ii, 52). "It is the law, not I, condemn your brother" (II. ii. 80). Perhaps even more reprehensible is Angelo's rejection of a crucial part of the Duke's commission to him in the opening scene of the play: "Mortality *and mercy* in Vienna/Live in thy tongue, and heart" (italics added).

During the course of their debate, Angelo, the man whom Lucio claims "never feels/The wanton stings and motions of the sense," succumbs to passion: "She speaks, and 'tis such sense/That my sense breeds with it" (II. ii. 142–43). Critics have argued that Angelo's sudden conversion from good to evil is not plausible, and that consistency of character demands the supposition that Shakespeare is presenting a hypocrite who gradually reveals himself. In my opinion, this interpretation is unsound. Angelo is not a hypocrite but only a man sadly lacking in self-knowledge. An examination of his soliloquy at the end of the scene shows that he is appalled at what he finds in himself: "What's this? What's this? Is this her fault, or mine?/The tempter, or the tempted, who sins most, ha?" (II. ii. 163–64). In traditional Renaissance fashion Angelo attributes his desire to pervert and destroy natural goodness to the workings of Satan: "O cunning enemy, that, to catch a saint,/With saints dost bait thy hook!" (II. ii. 180–81). And as if to make the point of his downfall even more poignant, Shakespeare lets him continue in the same vein the next time we see him: "When I would pray and think, I think and pray/To several subjects: Heaven hath my empty words,/Whilst my invention, hearing not my tongue,/Anchors on Isabel . . . ./Blood, thou are blood./Let's write good angel on the devil's horn—/'Tis not the devil's crest" (II. iv. 1–4, 15–17). The references to "blood" recall those by the Duke and Lucio in Act I. The angel/Angelo pun in juxtaposition with references to Satan likewise focusses the appearance/reality motif first emphasized by the Duke in Act I, scene iii.

When Isabella returns to Angelo's on the following day, she is faced with a different situation. Now the judge reveals himself as a lustful man who with inexorable logic breaks down Isabella's defense of Claudio. Why, if she wishes Claudio saved by bending the law, can she not bend her own sense of moral law and submit to Angelo's lust? Isabella can only repeat with variations that "lawful mercy/Is nothing kin to foul redemption" (II. iv. 112–13). Her argument is, in strictly logical terms, ineffectual, but Angelo's victory in the logical sphere is no triumph in the moral one. For it is her essential purity that, in modern idiom, perversely "turns him on."

Many critics[13] have censured Isabella for not trying to save Claudio by yielding to Angelo. The arguments raised against her are generally threefold: first, she is too harsh toward Claudio in Act III, scene i; second, she is too inflexible in her chastity; third, she taints herself by her participation in the Duke's bed-trick. On the other hand, Isabella has also had her defenders,[14] and in my own view they have the best of the argument. First of all, because absolute chastity is seen in a great deal of Renaissance literature as an absolute value. Contemporary defenses of such chastity can be found in Sir Thomas Elyot's *The Defence of Good Women* (1540), Castiglione's *The Book of the Courtier* (trans. Sir Thomas Hoby, 1561), Count Haniball Romei's *The Courtiers Academie* (trans. I[ohn] K[epers], London, 1598), Barnabe Rich's *The Excellency of Good Women* (1613), and in poems such as *The Faerie Queene* and *Comus*. In Shakespeare's major source of *Measure for Measure*, Whetstone's *Promos and Cassandra*, the loss of chastity is regarded by the heroine as an irreparable destruction of her honor and integrity.[15] Second, and more important, there is the evidence of Shakespeare's other plays, where chastity is always a supreme virtue in an unmarried woman, to be added to the

[13] See the article below by G. Wilson Knight and also the excerpt from Ernest Schanzer. Other significant attacks on Isabella in the twentieth century can be found in the following: F. R. Leavis, "The Greatness of 'Measure for Measure,'" *Scrutiny*, X (1942), 243; William Empson, "Sense in *Measure for Measure*," in *The Structure of Complex Words* (London, 1951), p. 279; J. W. Lever, ed. *Measure for Measure*, The Arden Shakespeare (London, 1965), pp. lxxi-lxxxiii; David Lloyd Stevenson, *The Achievement of Shakespeare's "Measure for Measure"* (Ithaca, N.Y., 1966), *passim*.

[14] See the article below by Elizabeth Marie Pope and the excerpt from R. W. Chambers, the finest defense of Isabella ever made. Much of what I say about Isabella here I have covered more fully in an essay, "Shakespeare's Isabella," to be published by *Shakespeare Quarterly*.

[15] See *Narrative and Dramatic Sources of Shakespeare*, ed. Geoffrey Bullough, II (London, 1958), 469, 498.

evidence of this play. The fact that he has made his heroine a novice
in a religious order (I. iv. 5, 9) can hardly have been calculated to
indicate anything other to an audience than that she will not and
should not yield. When Angelo tempts her and she replies: "Better it
were a brother died at once,/Than that a sister, by redeeming him,/
Should die for ever" (II. iv. 106–8), an audience with Christian training
could hardly avoid recalling scriptural injunctions against sins of the
flesh (1 Cor. vi: 9–10, 17–20, and Gal. v. 16–24) and the loss forever
of one's soul.

Isabella's rigid attitude toward chastity is theologically sound.
Moreover, the man whom practically all critics have acknowledged as
in some sense an emblem of upright authority in *Measure for Measure*
actually praises Isabella for the position she takes toward Claudio. The
Duke, overhearing Isabella berate Claudio for suggesting that she yield
her body to Angelo, says to her:

> The hand that hath made you fair hath made you good.
> The goodness that is cheap in beauty makes beauty
> brief in goodness; but grace, being the soul of your
> complexion, shall keep the body of it ever fair.
>
> (III. i. 179ff.)

Too little emphasis in the interpretation of *Measure for Measure* has
been placed upon this unequivocal statement. The Duke clearly
states that God has made Isabella attractive physically ("fair") and
upright morally ("good"). She, unlike Angelo, has a character in which
appearance and reality coincide. Her "complexion" ("external appearance" and also "temperament") is informed with Christian
"grace." In her, true physical beauty reflects true spiritual goodness.

As I read the play, Isabella is not to be thought of as excessive in
her refusal to give up her chastity to save Claudio (he himself asks her
pardon at III. i. 170), but only in the intensity, and possibly self-
righteousness, of her revulsion against his sin—a self-righteousness
she will transcend in the play's final scene. No more, in my view, is she
compromised by the Duke's bed-trick. As E. M. W. Tillyard points out,
the Duke makes all of the crucial decisions, moral and otherwise, after
his speech to Isabella in Act III, scene i,[16] and this is evidently dramatic
strategy to take the onus of hypocrisy off Isabella. The Friar-Duke's
justification of the bed-trick is to be accepted by the audience as Friar
Laurence's justification of the potion is accepted in *Romeo and Juliet*:
"the doubleness of the benefit [to both Isabella and Mariana] defends
the deceit from reproof" (III. i. 258–59). The Duke even repeats his
explanation twice more (at III. ii. 270–75 and IV. i. 71–76), lest any-

---

[16] See the excerpt from Tillyard below.

one in the audience misunderstand. Since most modern critics, even those who dislike Isabella, agree that the Duke has affinities with the Renaissance man who strives both for Socratic self-knowledge and Aristotelian temperance,[17] his sanction of the trick is strong evidence as to how it is to be viewed.

It has been argued that the Duke is a great teacher in *Measure for Measure*; he teaches "the properties of government," justice, and mercy; he supposedly even teaches Isabella "new wisdom" and the "wisdom of love." [18] Is this really the case? We know that he is testing Angelo, but I see no evidence that his object is also to teach Isabella, though it may well be that before she can plead for Angelo at the play's end she has learned a lesson. All that the Duke tells us is that he is keeping her in ignorance of Claudio's salvation "To make her heavenly comforts of despair/When it is least expected" (IV. iii. 109–10), but considering that she is a novice and that "grace" is "the soul" of her "complexion," the Duke's explanation is not as clear and detailed as we might like. Undoubtedly, Isabella is kept in ignorance *by Shakespeare* so that the theme of forgiveness can be dramatized in Act V. But the Duke does not say so. In fact, as the text of the play now stands, the Duke at best ambiguously suggests that he is testing Isabella to see if she will live up to his high esteem (V. i. 379–83, 489–90, 531–34) for her.

Once Angelo becomes committed to the rape of Isabella, the Duke leads him inexorably to exposure. In a spectacular public trial in Act V, he slowly strips away Angelo's defenses, then passes judgment upon the false judge in front of Isabella:

> . . . as he adjudg'd your brother,
> Being criminal in double violation
> Of sacred chastity and of promise-breach
> Thereon dependent, for your brother's life,
> The very mercy of the law cries out
> Most audible, even from his proper tongue:
> "An Angelo for Claudio; death for death.
> Haste still pays haste, and leisure answers leisure;
> Like doth quit like, and Measure still for Measure."
>   (V. i. 401–9)

Angelo's "double violation" is his assault against "sacred chastity" and his broken promise to Isabella to spare Claudio's life in return for her favors. The brilliant irony of the phrase "very mercy of the law" is evident when we recall Angelo's debates with Escalus and Isabella in

---

[17] As Escalus tells us, the Duke is one who "contended especially to know himself" and is "A gentleman of all temperance" (III.ii.226–31).

[18] See the articles by G. Wilson Knight and Francis Fergusson below.

Act II. The Old Testament doctrine of measure for measure that the
Duke applies to Angelo is likewise ironic, since Angelo once promised
Escalus that he would live by his own code of justice: "When I that
censure him [Claudio] do so offend,/Let mine own judgement pattern
out my death,/And nothing come in partial" (II. i. 29–31). For his
own part, Angelo's response to his exposure is certainly redemptive. He
has been publicly disgraced and yet has the courage of his earlier
convictions: "But let my trial be mine own confession./Immediate
sentence, then, and sequent death/Is all the grace I beg" (V. i. 370–72).
It is only after Isabella intercedes for Angelo, "Against all sense"
(V. i. 431), that the Duke produces Claudio and extends mercy and
pardon to everyone, including Angelo, Claudio, Lucio, and even the
condemned murderer Barnardine.

Critics have argued that Isabella's plea (V. i. 441–52) for Angelo is
too equivocal and legalistic to be considered truly Christian, but it is
more likely that her act is intended to reflect Christ's Sermon on the
Mount, evoked, as we have seen, from the very beginning of the play.[19]
Her ability to put into practice in Act V the Christian principles she
invokes in Act II shows how right the Duke is in saying of her: "The
hand that hath made you fair hath made you good." It is Isabella's
act of charity that gives impetus to the final series of pardons and
raises the ending of the play above theatrics.

III

The denouement of *Measure for Measure* is one of the major reasons
it has been termed a "problem play." Because of its realistic setting
and profound concern with ethical problems that at the close do not
seem to be solved in a properly serious way, E. M. W. Tillyard, for
instance, feels that it lacks internal harmony. Tillyard, in fact, locates
its structural flaw at III. i. 151, where the Duke steps in to mediate
between Claudio and Isabella. The structural break at this point
was first noted by F. S. Boas, who in 1896 became the first man to call
Measure for Measure, All's Well that Ends Well, Troilus and Cressida,
and *Hamlet* "problem plays." [20] Boas's terminology was probably
derived from the contemporary theater of Ibsen, Pinero, and H. A.
Jones. Although he never properly defined what he meant by "problem
play," Boas noted that *Hamlet* and *Troilus and Cressida* are character-

---

[19] See the excerpts below from Ernest Schanzer and Madeleine Doran. Schanzer's
opinion that Isabella has a "legalistic view of Divine Justice" is a somewhat
extreme articulation of Alfred Harbage's contention that the play's ending reveals
a "pragmatic . . . scheme of justice" (see *As They Liked It* [New York, 1947], p.
130). Miss Doran is, I think, closer to the spirit of the play with her emphasis
upon Isabella's forgiveness of Angelo.

[20] See *Shakspere and his Predecessors* (London, 1896), p. 345.

ized by "baffling obscurity" and *All's Well* and *Measure for Measure* by "perplexing moral entanglements" (p. 409).

The persistence of the term "problem play" is probably to be attributed to William Witherle Lawrence's study, *Shakespeare's Problem Comedies* (1931).[21] Following the lead of Boas, Lawrence once again grouped *Measure for Measure*, *All's Well*, and *Troilus and Cressida* as "problem plays" and defined the genre as one in which "a perplexing and distressing complication in human life is presented in a spirit of high seriousness" (p. 7). Moreover, in such a play "the theme is handled so as . . . to probe the complicated interrelations of character and action, in a situation admitting of different ethical interpretations" (p. 4). Ironically, Lawrence's whole essay on *Measure for Measure* seems designed to prove that knowledge of Elizabethan social mores and stage conventions leads us not to "different ethical interpretations" but to one "true interpretation of the whole play" (p. 121), which depends upon the realization that realistic and symbolic or conventional elements are combined throughout. Upon the whole, "problem play" is, in this writer's opinion, an unfortunate and confusing term. Originating with the kind of didactic "discussion" play that Ibsen and Shaw[22] wrote, it tends to make us think of Shakespeare's play as a sort of tract. Such an approach obscures outright its comic dimension and even, to some extent, its potentially tragic one. We might do well to bear in mind that in the First Folio of 1623 the play is placed with the comedies.

If the seriousness of the ethical issues raised makes it difficult today to view *Measure for Measure* as a comedy, the term "tragicomedy" is available. In a good, full-length study of the play, Mary Lascelles places it squarely in the tragicomic category and argues: "In tragicomedy, the concluding phase of the action is adjusted to meet our desire that those who are—at least by inclination and intention—good should neither suffer irreparable wrong nor be the cause of it to others . . . . To will, and to do, harm are, according to the logic of

[21] See the excerpt from Lawrence below.

[22] Shaw's ideas on "problem plays" are well-known but worth repeating. In the 1913 edition of *The Quintessence of Ibsenism* he pointed out that in modern drama "you have exposition, situation, and discussion; and the discussion is the test of the playwright"; in discussion lies "the real centre of . . . [the] play's interest." Modern audiences, he adds, want to see interesting plays: "Now an interesting play cannot in the nature of things mean anything but a play in which problems of conduct and character of personal importance to the audience are raised and suggestively discussed" ("The Technical Novelty in Ibsen's Plays," in *The Quintessence of Ibsenism* [London, 1926], pp. 187, 188, 190). W. W. Lawrence points out in the Preface to the second edition (1960) of his book that Shakespeare's "problem plays" are quite different from Ibsen's and require a different critical approach: ". . . Ibsen and Pinero started with the problem, and made action and character illustrate this, while Shakespeare started with old stories . . ." (p. v).

Shakespearian tragi-comedy, distinct; moreover, the doer of an ill act from which no harm results may share in the final amnesty." [23] Making the same point, J. W. Lever relates the play to Giambattista Guarini's *Compendio della poesia tragicomica,* first published separately in 1601 and then appended to Guarini's play *Il Pastor Fido* in 1602. The definition of tragicomedy in Guarini's *Compendium* seems altogether appropriate for what Shakespeare has accomplished in *Measure for Measure*: "He who composes tragicomedy takes from tragedy its great persons but not its great action, its verisimilar plot but not its true one, its movement of the feelings but not its disturbance of them, its pleasure but not its sadness, its danger but not its death; from comedy it takes laughter that is not excessive, modest amusement, feigned difficulty, happy reversal, and above all the comic order. . . ." [24] As Lever argues: "Whether or not Shakespeare had read Guarini's treatise, its ideas were in the air after 1602 and may well have prompted the design of *Measure for Measure,* with its blend of serious and comic, extreme peril and happy solution, mixed characters and 'well-tied knot.' " [25] The tragicomic genre, then, is able to accommodate both the serious deterministic world of tragedy and the humorous, indeterministic world of comedy. It is a genre peculiarly appropriate for a world in which false judges, libertines, virgins, erring adolescents, and sagacious elders can all coexist and at the same time share in a symbolic general reprieve, put forth under the rubric of mercy and forgiveness.

Measure for Measure is not in a technical sense one of Shakespeare's best plays, but in terms of the issues raised it is one of those most relevant to modern audiences. The problem of "government" in its relationship to law, license, justice, judgment, mercy, and morality is eternal and universal. The conflicts between the ruling philosophies of the lenient Duke and the strict Angelo can safely be seen in terms of modern problems of law enforcement, human freedom and responsibility, and social justice. Even the overwhelming preoccupation of *Measure for Measure* with sexual matters is appropriate for a mid–twentieth–century audience that is attempting to replace the Victorian standards of an Angelo without descending into the moral chaos implicit in the licentious world of Lucio and Pompey. Finally, and in the broadest sense, *Measure for Measure* speaks to "man, proud man," who, whether in office or not, "like an angry ape/Plays such fantastic tricks before high heaven/As makes the angels weep" (II. ii. 118, 121–23). In short, the play appeals to modern man in search of an identity and an enduring set of values.

---

[23] Mary Lascelles, *Shakespeare's "Measure for Measure"* (London, 1953), p. 157.
[24] Giambattista Guarini, "The Compendium of Tragicomic Poetry," trans. Allan H. Gilbert, in *Literary Criticism: Plato to Dryden* (Detroit, 1962), p. 511.
[25] Lever, p. lxii.

PART ONE

Background and Sources

Measure for Measure

by Kenneth Muir

The first literary treatment of the plot[1] of *Measure for Measure* was Claude Rouillet's *Philanira* (1556), a Latin play which was translated into French seven years later. This was followed in 1565 by the version given in Giraldi's *Hecatommithi*, a collection of tales in which Shakespeare also found the plot of *Othello*. There was a French translation by Gabriel Chappuys in 1584. Giraldi also wrote a dramatic version of the story, entitled *Epitia*, which was published posthumously in 1583; it was never acted. Meanwhile George Whetstone's play on the same theme, *Promos and Cassandra*, had been published in 1578, and this was Shakespeare's principal source. Three years later Thomas Lupton retold the story in the second part of *Siuquila*, and in 1582 Whetstone rehandled it as one of the tales in his *Heptameron of Civil Discourses*. There were other versions of the story, but they appear to have had no influence, direct or indirect, on Shakespeare's play.

It is probable that at the time he was working on *Othello* Shakespeare read the story of Epitia, and he may have read several of Giraldi's stories. From them, as Miss Mary Lascelles suggests,[2] he might have derived the idea of giving the story a happy ending, "of the inclination to pardon which is to be looked for in the man of highest authority," and of the capacity of the victim of intolerable wrong to forgive the villain when he is at her mercy.

In Giraldi's tale the Emperor Maximian leaves Juriste as his deputy

---

"Measure for Measure" *by Kenneth Muir. From* Shakespeare's Sources: I. Comedies and Tragedies *(London: Methuen & Co., Ltd., 1957, 1961, 1965), pp. 101–9. Reprinted by permission of the publisher.*
[1] Cf. Mary Lascelles, *Shakespeare's "Measure for Measure"* (1953), and the earlier studies, not altogether superseded, by F. E. Budd (*Revue de Littérature comparée*, 1931, pp. 711–36), by R. H. Ball (*University of Colorado Studies*, 1945, pp. 132–46), and by L. Albrecht (*Neue Untersuchungen zu Shakespeares Mass für Mass*, 1914).
[2] op. cit., p. 35.

to govern Innsbruck. Vico is condemned to death for rape. His sister, Epitia, urges Juriste to pardon him, and when she returns to hear his decision he offers to spare Vico if she yields to his lust, hinting that he may afterwards marry her. On Vico's entreaty, and on his arguing that marriage will repair the wrong, Epitia consents to Juriste's proposal, and on the morning afterwards Vico is executed and the body is sent to his sister. Epitia sets out to find the Emperor; Juriste is confronted with his victim and brought to confess; Epitia and Juriste are married forthwith, and she pleads with the Emperor to spare the life of the man who has wronged her. Epitia and Juriste live happily ever after. Here Shakespeare would have found the main outlines of his plot, though Isabella only pretends to assent to Angelo's proposal, Claudio's offence is not rape but fornication, and his life is spared by a trick, and although Isabella pleads for Angelo, she does not marry him.

From Giraldi's story, we may suppose, Shakespeare turned to Whetstone's long and rambling play, written for the most part in rhymed doggerel. Cassandra, a young and virtuous maiden, goes to Promos to beg her brother Andrugio's life, who has been condemned for rape—though there is some suggestion that the offence should rather be described as fornication. Promos agrees to pardon Andrugio and to marry Cassandra, on condition that she sleeps with him first. Andrugio pleads; she consents; but after she has carried out her side of the bargain,

> Promos, as feareles in promisse, as carelesse in performance, with sollemne vowe sygned her conditions: but worse than any Infydel, his will satisfyed, he performed neither the one nor the other: for to keepe his aucthoritie vnspotted with fauour, and to preuent *Cassandraes* clamors, he commaunded the Gayler secretly, to present *Cassandra* with her brother's head. The Gayler, with the outcryes of *Andrugio*, abhorring *Promos* lewdenes, by the prouidence of God, prouided thus for his safety. He presented *Cassandra* with a Felons head newlie executed, who . . . was so agreeued at this trecherye, that at the pointe to kyl her selfe, she spared that stroke to be auenged of *Promos*.

The Argument goes on to describe how she told the King her story; and he ordered that Promos should marry her and afterwards be executed.

> This maryage solempnised, *Cassandra* tyed in the greatest bonds of affection to her husband, became an earnest suter for his life.

The King refuses to grant her suit until the disguised Andrugio discloses his identity. Shakespeare certainly read the play, for he derived his idea of the underplot from it; but he also read Whetstone's narrative version, which in the *Heptameron* is recounted by one

Isabella. Miss Lascelles thinks[3] that Shakespeare may have read Lupton's version of the story, from which he could have got the idea of the disguised Prince, though in Middleton's *Phoenix*, acted perhaps before *Measure for Measure*, there is a disguised Prince who learns about the crimes and vices of society, and exposes them when he throws off his disguise. Lupton, however, hoped to legislate people into virtue, and he encouraged the use of informers. Shakespeare, if he read *Siuquila*, would have reacted violently against its spirit; and his reaction may have influenced his description of Angelo's rule in Vienna. Finally, there is more than a possibility that Shakespeare had read Giraldi's dramatic version, *Epitia*.[4]

[3] op. cit., pp. 22 ff., 36 ff.

[4] In addition to the critics mentioned . . . [elsewhere], Madeleine Doran, *Endeavors of Art* (1954), pp. 385–9, and E. Schanzer, privately, have discussed the possible indebtedness of Shakespeare to *Epitia*. Miss Doran has a convenient table of eight points in which *Measure for Measure* agrees with *Epitia* while diverging from the other sources. In two of these points, however, Giraldi's novel also agrees with *Epitia*. There remain: the name of Juriste's sister, Angela; the fact that the Secretary protests to the Podestà about the harshness of the law and the severity of its prosecution, and that he comments in soliloquy on the rigour of those in power; discussion in both plays of justice and mercy, power and authority; the substitution for Vico of a criminal hopelessly evil; the fact that Angela pleads with Epitia for Juriste's life, as Mariana does with Isabella, and that Epitia distinguishes between the act and the intention; and the fact that the Captain of the Prison announces that Vico has not been killed, as the Provost does in *Measure for Measure*, though Claudio, unlike Vico, comes on the stage.

Epitia tells the Emperor, as Isabella tells the Duke, that the sentence on her brother was just. The closest verbal parallels are the following:

> Oh, I wil to him, and plucke out his eies . . .
> Vnhappie *Claudio*, wretched *Isabell*,
> Iniurious world, most damned *Angelo*.
>   (IV. iii. 124, 126–7)
> Male ne hò detto à Iuriste, e poco meno
> Che non gli habbia cacciati ambiduo gli occhi,
> Accesa da giusta ira, e da vergogna . . .
>   (III. ii.)
> O scelerato, ò traditore Iuriste,
> O doloroso Epitia, ò miserella.
>   (III. i.)
> Whatsouer you may heare to the contrary, let Claudio
> be executed by foure of the clocke . . .
>   (IV. ii.)
> Andai al Podestà ratto, ei mostromme
> Lettra di man d'Iuriste, & del sigillo
> Di lui segnata, che gli commetteva
> Che, senza udir cosa, che fusse detta,
> Levar gli fesse il capo.

In the same scene is another reference to the hand and the seal:
> Lettra, segnata del maggior Sigillo.

Reading Giraldi's story or Whetstone's two versions, Shakespeare
would have been struck by the dramatic possibilities of the theme,
but he must have realized that the psychology of Cassandra was
theatrical and false. It is not easy to accept the spectacle of a virtuous
girl forgiving a man who is both her seducer and the supposed
murderer of her brother. Such a character could be interpreted only
in terms of psychopathology. The marriage at the end of the play
could be justified only if the character of Promos was whitewashed.
Shakespeare was therefore faced with two alternatives. He could make
a revenge-tragedy, ending the play with the death of the corrupt
deputy. Or, he could by various means mitigate the guilt of Promos,

---

Vincentio, in a different context, shows the Provost the hand and seal of the Duke.
As Ball says:

> The hand and seal, the letter with its order to disregard all other advice, the
> messenger, who is pictured arriving at the prison and bearing death when
> pardon is expected, are common only to *Epitia* and *Measure for Measure* and
> are not found in other sources.

The Emperor, on hearing Epitia's story, asks, "E questo è vero?" and she replies
"Più ver, che il vero." In the same way Vincentio tells Isabella "Nay, it is ten
times strange" and she replies:

> It is not truer he is Angelo
> Than this is all as true as it is strange.
> Nay, it is ten times true.

Later on Vincentio exclaims "This is most likely!" and Isabella again replies:

> O that it were as like as it is true.

Schanzer points out that Angela's maid soliloquizes on the power of a beautiful
young woman to obtain her petitions, and even take Jove's thunderbolt from his
hands:

> che potrà levare
> I fulmini di mano al sommo Giove
> Quando più fier, che mai fulmina, & tuona.

This may have suggested both Lucio's speech on the power of maidens (I. iv. 80-4)
and Isabella's speech beginning:

> Could great men thunder
> As *Ioue* himselfe do's . . .

In addition to some points already mentioned, Budd mentions three points of
resemblance: *Epitia*, like *Measure for Measure*, is a dissertation on justice; Epitia's
conduct may have suggested Vincentio's justification of his "pandering" for Angelo
and Mariana, that they were betrothed; and the Duke's speaking "on the adverse
side" at the opening of Angelo's trial finds a counterpart only in *Epitia*.
Some of these parallels are of doubtful validity; but the case that Shakespeare
had read *Epitia* is a strong one.

and so be able to end the play with his marriage. But both these solutions would have been comparatively feeble. He had already in *Titus Andronicus* written a revenge-play in which the guiltless heroine is raped, and the result is shocking rather than tragic. In *Lucrece* the heroine commits suicide. But it would not have been a satisfactory theme for a play, as we can see from the attempts of Heywood and Obey. On the other hand, however much the guilt of Promos were minimized, his marriage with the heroine would lay her open to the suspicion that she did not dislike his proposal as much as she pretended. To remove the suspicion altogether Shakespeare made his heroine a novice with a passionate hatred of sexual vice. He decided to write a play on the subject of forgiveness—not the forgiveness prompted by sexual passion as in Whetstone, nor even the magnanimity suggested in some of Giraldi's stories, but Christian forgiveness—that is, the forgiveness of enemies.

By making his heroine a novice Shakespeare made the conflict in her mind, whether she should agree to Angelo's proposal, as violent as possible; and this obviously added to the dramatic intensity of the plot. On the other hand, it meant, of course, that Isabella could not possibly consent to Angelo's proposal. As a Christian, and still more as a novice, she ought not to commit fornication even to save her brother's life; for if he demanded, or even accepted, the sacrifice, she would believe him to be damned. (She might, of course, have done it without telling him, like the heroine of Clemence Dane's *The Way Things Happen*; but there the man who is saved from prison is furious with the woman who has bought his freedom.) Yet Claudio's life had to be saved, so a substitute for Isabella had to be found. Already in the source a substitute on the block is found for Claudio; Shakespeare finds a substitute, Ragozine, for this substitute, Barnardine, and a substitute for Isabella in the shape of Mariana. The device was doubtless suggested by the plot of *All's Well*, in which Helena tricks Bertram in the same way, and from which the name Mariana is taken. The bed-trick, as it has been called, offends modern susceptibilities; but Shakespeare in both cases uses the situation to show how sexual passion blinds the victim. Bertram imagined that it would be distasteful to share a bed with his wife, and the summit of human felicity to share one with Diana; yet, as Helena comments:[5]

> O strange men,
> That can such sweet vse make of what they hate,
> When sawcie trusting of the cosin'd thoughts
> Defiles the pitchy night! So lust doth play
> With what it loathes, for that which is away.

[5] *A.W.* [*All's Well that Ends Well*] IV. iv. 21 ff.

Similarly Angelo imperils his immortal soul by offering to spare Claudio's life in exchange for a night with Isabella, and yet in the dark is unable to tell the difference between Isabella and Mariana.

Shakespeare, then, had to find a suitable substitute for Isabella. It had to be someone who loved Angelo and had some right to his bed. What better choice than someone to whom Angelo had been betrothed, and whom he had rejected for some reason appropriate to his character and to the theme of the play? The reason was not far to seek. Claudio, contracted to Juliet, had postponed the marriage ceremony for the sake of a dowry. Angelo, with far less excuse, had repudiated Mariana because her dowry had miscarried. Claudio's fornication, for which he is condemned to death, is shown to be less sinful than the mercenary behaviour of Angelo, though the latter earns a reputation for uprightness and self-control. It is necessary to the scheme of the play that Angelo should commit the very sin for which he had condemned another to death.

The fact that Isabella is a novice would suggest Angelo's character. He has to be something of a puritan. He is a man of severe morals, sincerely respected both by the Duke and Escalus. He believes himself to be proof against the temptation to commit sins of the flesh:[6]

> whose blood
> Is very snow-broth: one, who neuer feeles
> The wanton stings, and motions of the sence;
> But doth rebate, and blunt his naturall edge
> With profits of the minde: Studie, and fast . . .

They say this *Angelo* was not made by Man and Woman, after this downe-right way of Creation. . . . Some report, a Sea-maid spawn'd him. Some, that he was begot betweene two Stockfishes.

Shakespeare shows that chastity may proceed from meanness or cowardice. But it is wrong to regard Angelo as a villain. "He is betrayed by the subtler temptation which would mean nothing to a grosser man. He is moved by the sight of the beauty of a distressed woman's mind."[7] "His boasted self-control" (as Professor L. C. Knights has shown[8]) "is not only a matter of conscious will, but of a will taut and strained." "Once the precarious balance is upset," he is betrayed by the sexual instinct he despised. As Cadoux puts it:[9] "His scheme of life has no decent place for sex, and therefore no foothold from which to fight its indecencies." The puritanical streak in Angelo's character

---

[6] *M.M.* I. iv: 57 ff.; III. ii. 97 ff.

[7] J. Masefield, *William Shakespeare* (1911), p. 178.

[8] *Scrutiny*, X (1942), p. 222–33.

[9] A. T. Cadoux, *Shakespearean Selves* (1938), p. 81.

may have been suggested by the self-righteous and rigid attitude displayed by Lupton.

Until recently most critics have objected to Isabella's forgiveness of Angelo. Johnson and Coleridge for once were in agreement, and Bridges[10] thought the ending showed a lack of artistic conscience. Professor W. W. Lawrence excuses Shakespeare by saying[11] that it was customary in the drama of the period for the repentant villain to be married to the heroine. But Angelo, though he is morally guilty of lust and murder and actually guilty of hypocrisy, meanness, and treachery, is not really a villain; he is a "sincere self-deceiver," as Mr. J. I. M. Stewart says,[12] the kind of person who is "liable to the kind of aberration depicted." Angelo, moreover, is not the central character of the play, and those recent critics who have justified the ending of the play have done so by showing that Isabella, who had pleaded with Angelo for her brother, is put in the position where she is called upon to forgive the man who has wronged her. She passes this test of the sincerity of her religion—a test which has been imposed by the Duke—after an agonizing struggle.

Shakespeare, by making his heroine a novice, involves Claudio also in a searching ordeal; and by making his Duke return in disguise to manipulate the action, he ensures that the characters shall be tempted without tragic results. Even Barnardine is spared, and only Lucio, who in spite of his corrupt charm is a cold-hearted lecher, informer, and slanderer, is treated with some severity. It is difficult to agree with Professor Ellis-Fermor that[13] "the lowest depths of Jacobean cynicism" are touched in this play. Many of the minor characters are depicted sympathetically—the warm, forgiving Mariana, the humane Provost, the saintly Juliet. Shakespeare, indeed, was not without sympathy for Pompey the pimp, for Barnardine the drunken murderer, and for Mistress Overdone the bawd who looks after Lucio's bastard.

Dr. Tillyard complains,[14] with greater justice, that the play falls into two disparate halves. After the scene between Claudio and Isabella most of the play is in prose, and what poetry there is, is greatly inferior to that of the first two acts. Theatrical intrigue takes the place of psychological profundity and great poetry. Dr. Tillyard is right to point out the change in the second half of the play, but apart from the fact that the last two acts are highly successful on the stage, they may be defended on more respectable grounds. It is the interven-

---

[10] R. Bridges, *The Influence of the Audience* (1927), p. 13.
[11] op. cit. [*Shakespeare's Problem Comedies* (1931)], p. 116.
[12] *Character and Motive in Shakespeare* (1949), pp. 14, 141.
[13] *The Jacobean Drama* (1936), p. 263.
[14] *Shakespeare's Problem Plays* (1950), p. 132.

tion of the Divine in human affairs which transforms the style and
pattern in the second half of the play. The characters become puppets,
"taking part in no common action," [15] and manipulated so that they
all find judgement or salvation. In the first part of the play the characters blunder along in their human way, until they can be saved only
by Providence Divine. Thereafter they are whirled about so swiftly
that they do not have any time, even for poetry. The poetry is in the
action itself.

[15] T. S. Eliot, *Murder in the Cathedral*. It may be added, as I have suggested elsewhere (*N.Q.* [*Notes and Queries*], 1956, p. 424), that a few minor details in *Measure
for Measure* seem to have been derived from one of Erasmus's *Colloquia*. Shakespeare
may have consulted the "Funus" to obtain background information about friars
and nuns. Erasmus tells us that a dying man's younger son is dedicated to St.
Francis, his elder daughter to St. Clare (ed. 1571, p. 503: *Filius minor dicaretur S.
Fransisco, filia maior S. Clarae*). This passage may have suggested making Isabella
a votaress of St. Clare, as the dative *Fransisco* suggested Francisca, Isabella's inter-
locutor. Nor is this all. In the same context Erasmus tells us that the dying man
is visited by Bernardine, a Franciscan friar, and Vincentius, a Dominican friar. On
the page next to the one which contains the reference to St. Clare, Erasmus speaks
of *Barnardino, tantundem Vincentio*. Here the misprint for *Bernardino* and the
case in which Vincentius appears seem to have suggested the names Barnardine and
Vincentio. William Burton's translation of seven of the *Colloquies*, including the
"Funus," did not appear until 1606, after the first performance of *Measure for
Measure*.

The Disguised Ruler

by J. W. Lever

Rulers in disguise became popular figures on the stage, as in *Fair Em, A Knack to Know a Knave, George a Greene,* and Part I of *Sir John Oldcastle.*[1] Shakespeare's Henry V plays a similar part on the eve of the Battle of Agincourt. In Rowley's *When You See Me You Know Me,* Henry VIII wanders by night through the disreputable quarters of London, encountering constables and watchmen of much the same type as Dogberry, Verges, or Elbow. Such episodes provided light entertainment in an English setting; but with the advent of a new satirical trend in Jacobean drama, a more sophisticated approach came into fashion. Marston's *The Malcontent* and *Fawn,* and Middleton's *Phoenix,* presented fictitious Italian dukes who put off their conventional dignity with their robes of state and gave strident expression to the contemporary questioning of values.[2] There was bitter railing against the vices of court and country, but Puritan zeal was equally castigated and the disguised dukes showed none of the ruthless rectitude which had endeared Severus* to radical reformers. The titular hero of *The Malcontent,* his personality split between the dual roles of the scurrilous Malevole and the noble Altofronto, finally emerges as the model Christian-Stoic ruler who disdains to take revenge on his enemies, embraces his true friends, and reaffirms his love for his wife.

Dissociated from reformist publicity, the legend of the Disguised Ruler had thus become a flexible literary device. It served for romance, for light comedy, for popular "exposures" of low life and, in the early

---

"The Disguised Ruler" by J. W. Lever. From the Introduction to Measure for Measure, *The Arden Shakespeare Series,* ed. J. W. Lever (London: Methuen & Co., Ltd., 1965), pp. xlvii–li. Reprinted by permission of the publisher.

[1] See V. O. Freeburg, *Disguise Plots in Elizabethan Drama* (1915), chap. 7; M. C. Bradbrook, "Shakespeare and the Use of Disguise in Elizabethan Drama," *Essays In Criticism,* II (1952), 159–68.

[2] On the relationship of these plays to *Measure for Measure,* see W. W. Lawrence, *Shakespeare's Problem Comedies* (1931), 215; O. J. Campbell, *Shakespeare's Satire* (1943), 127; and Lascelles, 26–7.

* [Alexander Severus was a Roman emperor frequently mentioned by Renaissance moralists.—ED.]

years of the new century, for a more critical, self-wounding expression
of social malaise. In its most serious form it confirmed the central
humanist concept of royal authority, according to which the true
ruler set an example of wisdom, temperance, and magnanimity:

> Princes, that would their people should doe well,
> Must at themselves begin, as at the head;
> For men, by their example, patterne out
> Their imitations, and reguard of lawes:
> A vertuous *Court* a world to vertue drawes.[3]

These familiar notions, and the Disguised Ruler theme itself,
acquired fresh topicality with the accession of James I. Described as "a
Living Library, and a walking Study," [4] James sought in his discourse
and public utterances to present himself as a philosopher-king who
shaped his actions according to the best models of Christian humanism.
His *Basilicon Doron* was at once a text-book of political ethics and a
statement of personal aims. In forthright, idiomatic style it referred to
the author's own experiences as a ruler; to his difficulties, his mistakes,
and the lessons he had learned, as well as to the moral principles on
which he based his private life.

The view that Shakespeare's Duke was deliberately modelled on the
personality of King James was first suggested by Chalmers, and argued
at length by Albrecht, who treated *Basilicon Doron* as a direct source
of *Measure for Measure*. Similar claims have been put forward more
recently in an important article by David L. Stevenson, and supported
by Ernest Schanzer in his study of the play.[5] These writers overlook
the shaping factor of the Severus legend, but the case for some measure
of identification is too strong to be discounted. Shakespeare and his
company, honoured and patronized by the new king, could hardly have
been impervious to the political atmosphere of the time or quite
uninfluenced by the most widely discussed book of 1603. Two principles
at least, as set forth in *Basilicon Doron,* are given prominence in
Measure for Measure. One was the duty of rulers to display virtue in
action:

> So to glister and shine before their people . . . that their persons as
> brighte lampes of godlines and vertue may . . . give light to all their
> steppes . . .

[3] Ben Jonson, *Cynthia's Revels*, concluding lines.
[4] William Barlow, *The Summe and Substance of the Conference . . . at Hampton
Court* (1604), 84. (Cited by Stevenson, *E.L.H.* [*English Literary History*] XXVI
(1959), 200.)
[5] Edward Chalmers, *A Supplemental Apology for the Believers in the Shake-
speare-Papers* (1799), 404–5; Albrecht, *op. cit.* [*Neue Untersuchungen zu Shake-
peares Mass für Mass*, 1914], *passim;* David L. Stevenson, *loc. cit.*, 188–208: Ernest
Schanzer, *The Problem Plays of Shakespeare* (1963), 120–5.

it is not ynough that ye have and retaine (as prisoners) within your selfe never so many good qualities and vertues, except that ye imploy them, and set them on worke . . .[6]

To audiences of 1604 the Duke's initial advice to Angelo

> Heaven doth with us as we with torches do,
> Not light them for themselves; for if our virtues
> Did not go forth of us, 'twere all alike
> As if we had them not   (I. i. 32–5)

and the opening lines of the Duke's soliloquy at the end of Act III must necessarily have recalled the king's precepts. Of equal importance was the principle of temperance, or the Aristotelean mean, as the chief of virtues:

> make . . . Temperance, Queene of all the rest within you. I meane . . . that wise moderation, that first commanding your selfe, shall as a Queene, command all the affections & passions of your minde . . . even in your most vertuous actions, make ever moderation to be the chief ruler. For although holinesse be the first and most requisite qualitie of a Christian, yet . . . moderate all your outward actions flowing there-fra. The like say I nowe of Iustice . . . otherwaies *summum ius*, is *summa iniuria* . . . For lawes are ordained as rules of vertuous and sociall living, and not to be snares to trap your good subiectes: and therefore the lawe must be interpreted according to the meaning, and not to the literall sense . . . And as I said of Iustice, so say I of Clemencie . . . *Nam in medio stat virtus* (pp. 137–43).

There could hardly be a more apt comment on the attitudes of the Duke, Angelo, and Isabella in Shakespeare's play. Besides James's general principles, a number of his personal traits went to the making of the Duke. James admitted in *Basilicon Doron* that he had ruled too laxly at the beginning of his reign:[7] similarly the Duke, without precedent either in the fictional sources or any version of the Severus story, confessed " 'twas my fault to give the people scope" (I.iii). Again, James I's over-sensitive reaction to calumny,[8] and his desire that the laws should be put into execution against "unreverent speakers," are matched in the Duke's complaint against "back-wounding calumny" and his exceptionally severe rebukes to Lucio in the last act. With inverse effect, Lucio's slanders about the Duke's sexual morals form a

---

[6] *B.D.*, 27, 61 (1603 text). James's views were largely traditional; but the personal approach and the work's topicality suggest that it had a more direct influence than earlier writings.

[7] P. 31.

[8] "the malice of the children of envy" (*B.D.*, 13); also 32–3, 52–3, 72, 93, and elsewhere.

ridiculous contrast to the king's earnest warnings against the sin of fornication.[9]

James's actions as well as his opinions may also have had their influence on Shakespeare's conception of the Duke. As often, life approximated to current trends in literature, and a romantic streak in the king's temperament would seem to explain his attempts to play the part of a Severus. He could not walk the streets of London disguised as a merchant; but his would-be secret visit to the Exchange in March 1604, with the object of watching the merchants while remaining unobserved, was an adventure in much the same spirit.[10] James also sought to imitate legendary rulers in exemplary acts of justice. A celebrated occasion was the trial at Newark in April 1603, when the king in person sentenced a pickpocket to death but amnestied all the prisoners in the tower, thus demonstrating that justice should be combined with mercy.[11] Robert A. Shedd has cited an even more striking example of the "Severus touch" at Winchester in the winter of 1603–4 in connexion with the Raleigh conspiracy.[12] After a number of executions, James resolved upon a striking and carefully timed display of mercy. On the very morning fixed for the execution of a group of conspirators, a letter with the royal countermand was secretly conveyed to the sheriff. The prisoners were actually brought out to the scaffold, expecting immediate death; taken back without explanation; and at last recalled to hear a speech on the heinousness of treason and the surpassing mercy of the monarch who had pardoned their lives. This time the king's *coup de théâtre* was an unqualified success:

> There was no need to beg a *plaudite* of the audience, for it was given with such hues and cries that it went forth from the Castle into the town and there began afresh . . . And this experience was made of the difference of examples of justice and mercy, that . . . no man could cry loud enough, "God save the King!"[13]

To see the Duke in *Measure for Measure* as an exact replica of James I would be to misunderstand both Shakespeare's dramatic methods and the practice of the contemporary stage. But to suppose that no parallel was to be drawn between the two characters, or that,

---

[9] "thought but a light & veniall sinne, by the most part of the world: yet . . . count euerie sinne . . . as God . . . accounteth of the same" (*B.D.* 123).

[10] See above, pp. xxxiii–xxxv.

[11] See *A Jacobean Journal*, ed. G. B. Harrison (1941), 15.

[12] In "The *Measure for Measure* of Shakespeare's 1604 Audience" (unpublished dissertation, Univ. of Michigan 1953, typescript 172 ff.).

[13] Lucy Aikin, *Memoirs of the Court of King James the First* (1822, 2 vols.), 1. 174 (cited by Shedd).

according to the familiar formula, "any resemblance to any living person was purely accidental," would seem to be just as untenable.[14] In times when real life took on the properties of legend, it was likely enough that the chief playwright of the King's Men should find fresh relevance in the theme of the Disguised Ruler, and that a vital link between the disparate personalities of Severus and Maximian* should be perceived in the character of the new sovereign.

While the story of the Corrupt Magistrate became in *Measure for Measure* a study of conflicting persons and principles, that of the Disguised Ruler served to erect a norm as well as an active force reconciling opposites through moderation and virtue. Between the extremes of justice and mercy, holiness and vice, tyranny and licence, stood the Duke, "a gentleman of all temperance," exemplifying what most of Shakespeare's contemporaries would regard as the model ruler of a Christian polity. As a foil to the Duke, Lucio may well have been suggested by Riche's slanderous courtier.† At the same time Lucio bore a generic likeness to the garrulous, ebullient Parolles of *All's Well That Ends Well*, and suitably typified the "pretended gallants, banckrouts and vnruly youths . . . at this time setled in pyracie"[15] who clamoured against the peace policy of the new king. In his dialogue with the Duke, Lucio provided a necessary dramatic counterpoint. Whereas Marston's Altofronto had to assume the fantastic personality of Malevole in order to rail effectively at the corruption of the times, Shakespeare projected some of his satire through a second character, whose scurrility balanced the apparent conformism of the Duke in his guise of friar. Finally, it is possible that Angelo derived his distinctive personality not only from the traditional "corrupt magistrate," but also from those traits in James's Puritan adversaries which the king hit off by contraries in the conclusion to Book 1 of *Basilicon Doron:*

> Keepe God more sparingly in your mouth, but aboundantly in your hart:[16] be precise in effect, but sociall in shew: kythe more by your deedes then by your wordes the love of vertue & hatred of vice: and delight more to be godlie and verteous in deed, then to be thought and

---

[14] Schanzer writes: "I think . . . that it is an idealized image, made up of the qualities in a ruler which James had particularly praised; and that it is yet sufficiently particularized, and endowed with traits peculiar to the King, to enable Shakespeare's audience and James himself to recognize the likeness" (*The Problem Plays of Shakespeare* (1963), 123).

* [The Emperor in G. B. Giraldi Cinthio's tale.—ED.]

† [Barnabe Riche's *The Adventures of Brusanus, Prince of Hungaria* (1952) contains an analogue to Shakespeare's play.—ED.]

[15] John Stow, *op. cit.* [*Annales,* 1615], 845. See above, pp. xxxi–xxxii.

[16] Cf. II. iv. 4–7.

called so; . . . inwardly garnished with true Christian humilitie, not
outwardly (with the proud Pharisee) glorying in your godlinesse: . . .
And . . . ye shall eschew outwardly before the worlde, the suspition of
filthie proud hypocrisie and deceitfull dissimulation.[17]

[17] *B.D.*, 20-1.

PART TWO

Interpretations

Measure for Measure and the Gospels

by G. Wilson Knight

In *Measure for Measure* we have a careful dramatic pattern, a studied explication of a central theme: the moral nature of man in relation to the crudity of man's justice, especially in the matter of sexual vice. There is, too, a clear relation existing between the play and the Gospels, for the play's theme is this:

Judge not, that ye be not judged. For with what judgment ye judge, ye shall be judged: and with what measure ye mete, it shall be measured to you again. (Matthew, vii. 1)

The ethical standards of the Gospels are rooted in the thought of *Measure for Measure.* Therefore, in this analysis we shall, while fixing attention primarily on the play, yet inevitably find a reference to the New Testament continually helpful, and sometimes essential.

Measure for Measure is a carefully constructed work. Not until we view it as a deliberate artistic pattern of certain pivot ideas determining the play's action throughout shall we understand its peculiar nature. Though there is consummate psychological insight here and at least one person of most vivid and poignant human interest, we must first have regard to the central theme, and only second look for exact verisimilitude to ordinary processes of behaviour. We must be careful not to let our human interest in any one person distort our single vision of the whole pattern. The play tends towards allegory or symbolism. The poet elects to risk a certain stiffness, or arbitrariness, in the directing of his plot rather than fail to express dramatically, with variety and precision, the full content of his basic thought. Any stiffness in the matter of human probability is, however, more than balanced by its extreme fecundity and compacted significance of dramatic symbolism. The persons of the play tend to illustrate certain human qualities chosen with careful reference to the

"Measure for Measure *and the Gospels" by G. Wilson Knight. From* The Wheel of Fire *(London: Methuen & Co., Ltd., 1930; 4th rev. ed., 1949), pp. 73–96. Reprinted by permission of the publisher.*

main theme. Thus Isabella stands for sainted purity, Angelo for
Pharisaical righteousness, the Duke for a psychologically sound and
enlightened ethic. Lucio represents indecent wit, Pompey and Mistress
Overdone professional immorality. Barnadine is hard-headed, criminal, insensitiveness. Each person illumines some facet of the central
theme: man's moral nature. The play's attention is confined chiefly
to sexual ethics: which in isolation is naturally the most pregnant of
analysis and the most universal of all themes. No other subject provides so clear a contrast between human consciousness and human
instinct; so rigid a distinction between the civilized and the natural
qualities of man; so amazing, yet so slight, a boundary set in the
public mind between the foully bestial and the ideally divine in
humanity. The atmosphere, purpose, and meaning of the play are
throughout ethical. The Duke, lord of this play in the exact sense
that Prospero is lord of *The Tempest,* is the prophet of an enlightened
ethic. He controls the action from start to finish, he allots, as it were,
praise and blame, he is lit at moments with divine suggestion comparable with his almost divine power of fore-knowledge, and control,
and wisdom. There is an enigmatic, other-worldly, mystery suffusing
his figure and the meaning of his acts: their results, however, in each
case justify their initiation—wherein we see the allegorical nature of
the play, since the plot is so arranged that each person receives his
deserts in the light of the Duke's—which is really the Gospel—ethic.
   The poetic atmosphere is one of religion and critical morality. The
religious colouring is orthodox, as in *Hamlet.* Isabella is a novice
among "the votarists of St. Clare" (I. iv. 5); the Duke disguises himself as a Friar, exercising the divine privileges of his office towards
Juliet, Barnadine, Claudio, Pompey. We hear of "the consecrated
fount a league below the city" (IV. iii. 106). The thought of death's
eternal damnation, which is prominent in *Hamlet,* recurs in Claudio's
speech:

> Ay, but to die and go we know not where;
> To lie in cold obstruction and to rot;
> This sensible warm motion to become
> A kneaded clod; and the delighted spirit
> To bathe in fiery floods, or to reside
> In thrilling region of thick-ribbed ice;
> To be imprison'd in the viewless winds,
> And blown with restless violence round about
> The pendant world; or to be worse than worst
> Of those that lawless and incertain thoughts
> Imagine howling: 'tis too horrible!
> The weariest and most loathed worldly life

> That age, ache, penury, and imprisonment
> Can lay on nature is a paradise
> To what we fear in death.   (III. i. 116)

So powerful can orthodox eschatology be in *Measure for Measure*:
it is not, as I shall show, all-powerful. Nor is the play primarily a
play of death-philosophy: its theme is rather that of the Gospel ethic.
And there is no more beautiful passage in all Shakespeare on the Christian redemption than Isabella's lines to Angelo:

> Alas! Alas!
> Why, all the souls that were, were forfeit once;
> And He, that might the vantage best have took,
> Found out the remedy. How would you be,
> If He which is the top of judgement, should
> But judge you as you are? O, think on that;
> And mercy then will breathe within your lips,
> Like man new made.   (II. ii. 72)

This is the natural sequence to Isabella's earlier lines:

> Well, believe this,
> No ceremony that to great ones 'longs,
> Not the king's crown, nor the deputed sword,
> The marshal's truncheon, nor the judge's robe,
> Become them with one half so good a grace
> As mercy does.   (II. ii. 58)

These thoughts are a repetition of those in Portia's famous "mercy"
speech. There they come as a sudden, gleaming, almost irrelevant
beam of the ethical imagination. But here they are not irrelevant:
they are intrinsic with the thought of the whole play, the pivot of
its movement. In *The Merchant of Venice* the Gospel reference is
explicit:

> . . . We do pray for mercy;
> And that same prayer doth teach us all to render
> The deeds of mercy.   (IV. i. 200)

And the central idea of *Measure for Measure* is this:

And forgive us our debts as we forgive our debtors (Matthew, vi, 12).

Thus "justice" is a mockery: man, himself a sinner, cannot presume
to judge. That is the lesson driven home in *Measure for Measure*.

The atmosphere of Christianity pervading the play merges into
the purely ethical suggestion implicit in the inter-criticism of all the
persons. Though the Christian ethic be the central theme, there is a

wider setting of varied ethical thought, voiced by each person in turn,
high or low. The Duke, Angelo, and Isabella are clearly obsessed
with such ideas and criticize freely in their different fashions. So also
Elbow and the officers bring in Froth and Pompey, accusing them.
Abhorson is severely critical of Pompey:

> A bawd? Fie upon him! He will discredit our mystery.
>
> (IV. ii. 29)

Lucio traduces the Duke's character, Mistress Overdone informs
against Lucio. Barnadine is universally despised. All, that is, react
to each other in an essentially ethical mode: which mode is the
peculiar and particular vision of this play. Even music is brought to
the bar of the ethical judgement:

> . . . music oft hath such a charm
> To make bad good, and good provoke to harm.
>
> (IV. i. 16)

Such is the dominating atmosphere of this play. Out of it grow the
main themes, the problem and the lesson of *Measure for Measure*.
There is thus a pervading atmosphere of orthodoxy and ethical
criticism, in which is centred the mysterious holiness, the profound
death-philosophy, the enlightened human insight and Christian ethic
of the protagonist, the Duke of Vienna.

The satire of the play is directed primarily against self-conscious,
self-protected righteousness. The Duke starts the action by resigning
his power to Angelo. He addresses Angelo, outspoken in praise of his
virtues, thus:

> Angelo,
> There is a kind of character in thy life,
> That to the observer doth thy history
> Fully unfold. Thyself and thy belongings
> Are not thine own so proper, as to waste
> Thyself upon thy virtue, they on thee.
> Heaven doth with us as we with torches do;
> Not light them for themselves; for if our virtues
> Did not go forth of us, 'twere all alike
> As if we had them not. Spirits are not finely touch'd,
> But to fine issues, nor Nature never lends
> The smallest scruple of her excellence,
> But, like a thrifty goddess, she determines
> Herself the glory of a creditor,
> Both thanks and use.   (I. i. 27)

The thought is similar to that of the Sermon on the Mount:

> Ye are the light of the world. A city that is set on an hill cannot be hid.
> Neither do men light a candle, and put it under a bushel, but on a
> candlestick; and it giveth light unto all that are in the house.
>
> (Matthew, v. 14)

Not only does the Duke's "torch" metaphor clearly recall this passage,
but his development of it is vividly paralleled by other of Jesus' words.
The Duke compares "Nature" to "a creditor," lending qualities and
demanding both "thanks and use." Compare:

> For the Kingdom of Heaven is as a man travelling into a far country,
> who called his own servants, and delivered unto them his goods.
>
> And unto one he gave five talents, to another two, and to another
> one; to every man according to his several ability; and straightway
> took his journey. (Matthew, xxv. 14)

The sequel needs no quotation. Now, though Angelo modestly refuses
the honour, the Duke insists, forcing it on him. Later, in conversation
with Friar Thomas, himself disguised as a Friar now, he gives us
reason for his strange act:

> We have strict statutes and most biting laws,
> The needful bits and curbs to headstrong steeds,
> Which for this nineteen years we have let slip;
> Even like an o'ergrown lion in a cave,
> That goes not out to prey. Now, as fond fathers,
> Having bound up the threatening twigs of birch,
> Only to stick it in their children's sight
> For terror, not to use, in time the rod
> Becomes more mock'd than fear'd; so our decrees,
> Dead to infliction, to themselves are dead;
> And liberty plucks justice by the nose;
> The baby beats the nurse, and quite athwart
> Goes all decorum. (I. iii. 19)

Therefore he has given Angelo power and command to "strike home."
Himself he will not exact justice, since he has already, by his laxity,
as good as bade the people sin by his "permissive pass": the people
could not readily understand such a change in himself—with a new
governor it would be different. But these are not his only reasons.
He ends:

> Moe reasons for this action
> At our more leisure shall I render you;
> Only, this one: Lord Angelo is precise;
> Stands at a guard with envy; scarce confesses

> That his blood flows, or that his appetite
> Is more to bread than stone: hence shall we see
> If power change purpose, what our seemers be.
>   (I. iii. 48)

The rest of the play slowly unfolds the rich content of the Duke's plan, and the secret, too, of his lax rule.

Escalus tells us that the Duke was

> One that, above all other strifes, contended especially to know himself.
>   (III. ii. 252)

But he has studied others, besides himself. He prides himself on his knowledge:

> There is written in your brow, provost, honesty and constancy: if I read it not truly, my ancient skill beguiles me . . .   (IV. ii. 161)

Herein are the causes of his leniency. His government has been inefficient, not through an inherent weakness or laxity in him, but rather because meditation and self-analysis, together with profound study of human nature, have shown him that all passions and sins of other men have reflected images in his own soul. He is no weakling: he has been "a scholar, a statesman, and a soldier" (III. ii. 158). But to such a philosopher government and justice may begin to appear a mockery, and become abhorrent. His judicial method has been original: all criminals were either executed promptly or else freely released (IV. ii. 136–9). Nowhere is the peculiar modernity of the Duke in point of advanced psychology more vividly apparent. It seems, too, if we are to judge by his treatment of Barnadine (IV. iii. 71–88), that he could not tolerate an execution without the criminal's own approval! The case of Barnadine troubles him intensely:

> A creature unprepared, unmeet for death;
> And to transport him in the mind he is
> Were damnable.   (IV. iii. 74)

The Duke's sense of human responsibility is delightful throughout: he is like a kindly father, and all the rest are his children. Thus he now performs the experiment of handing the reins of government to a man of ascetic purity who has an hitherto invulnerable faith in the rightness and justice of his own ideals—a man of spotless reputation and self-conscious integrity, who will have no fears as to the "justice" of enforcing precise obedience. The scheme is a plot, or trap: a scientific experiment to see if extreme ascetic righteousness can stand the test of power.

The Duke, disguised as the Friar, moves through the play, a dark

figure, directing, watching, moralizing on the actions of the other
persons. As the play progresses and his plot on Angelo works he
assumes an ever-increasing mysterious dignity, his original purpose
seems to become more and more profound in human insight, the
action marches with measured pace to its appointed and logical end.
We have ceased altogether to think of the Duke as merely a studious
and unpractical governor, incapable of office. Rather he holds, within
the dramatic universe, the dignity and power of a Prospero, to whom
he is strangely similar. With both, their plot and plan is the plot
and plan of the play: they make and forge the play, and thus are
automatically to be equated in a unique sense with the poet himself—
since both are symbols of the poet's controlling, purposeful, combined,
movement of the chess-men of the drama. Like Prospero, the Duke
tends to assume proportions evidently divine. Once he is actually compared to the Supreme Power:

> O my dread lord,
> I should be guiltier than my guiltiness,
> To think I can be undiscernible,
> When I perceive your grace, like power divine,
> Hath look'd upon my passes.   (V. i. 367)

So speaks Angelo at the end. We are prepared for it long before. In
the rhymed octosyllabic couplets of the Duke's soliloquy in III. ii.
there is a distinct note of supernatural authority, forecasting the
rhymed mystic utterances of divine beings in the Final Plays. He has
been talking with Escalus and the Provost, and dismisses them with
the words:

> Peace be with you!

They leave him and he soliloquizes:

> He who the sword of heaven will bear
> Should be as holy as severe;
> Pattern in himself to know
> Grace to stand and virtue go;
> More nor less to other paying
> Than by self-offences weighing.
> Shame to him whose cruel striking
> Kills for faults of his own liking!
> Twice treble shame on Angelo,
> To weed my vice and let his grow!
> O what may man within him hide,
> Though angel on the outward side!
> How may likeness made in crimes,

> Making practice on the times,
> To draw with idle spiders' strings
> Most ponderous and substantial things!
> Craft against vice I must apply:
> With Angelo to-night shall lie
> His old betrothed but despised;
> So disguise shall, by the disguised,
> Pay with falsehood false exacting,
> And perform an old contracting.
>
>   (III. ii. 283)

This fine soliloquy gives us the Duke's philosophy: the philosophy
that prompted his original plan. And it is important to notice the
mystical, prophetic tone of the speech.

The Duke, like Jesus, is the prophet of a new order of ethics. This
aspect of the Duke as teacher and prophet is also illustrated by his
cryptic utterance to Escalus just before this soliloquy:

> *Escalus.* Good even, good father.
> *Duke.* Bliss and goodness on you.
> *Escalus.* Of whence are you?
> *Duke.* Not of this country, though my chance is now
>   To use it for my time: I am a brother
>   Of gracious order, late come from the See
>   In special business from his Holiness.
> *Escalus.* What news abroad i' the world?
> *Duke.* None, but that there is so great a fever on goodness, that the
>   dissolution of it must cure it: novelty is only in request; and it as
>   dangerous to be aged in any kind of course, as it is virtuous to be
>   constant in any undertaking. There is scarce truth enough alive to make
>   societies secure; but security enough to make fellowships accurst: much
>   upon this riddle runs the wisdom of the world. This news is old
>   enough, yet it is every day's news. I pray you, sir, of what disposition
>   was the Duke?
> *Escalus.* One that, above all other strifes, contended especially to know
>   himself.
>
>   (III. ii. 233)

This remarkable speech, with its deliberate, incisive, cryptic sentences,
has a profound quality and purpose which reaches the very heart of
the play. It deserves exact attention. Its expanded paraphrase runs
thus:

> No news, but that goodness is suffering such a disease that a complete
> dissolution of it (goodness) is needed to cure it. That is, our whole
> system of conventional ethics should be destroyed and rebuilt. A change
> (novelty) never gets beyond request, that is, is never actually put in

practice. And it is as dangerous to continue indefinitely a worn-out system or order of government, as it is praiseworthy to be constant in any individual undertaking. There is scarcely enough knowledge of human nature current in the world to make societies safe; but ignorant self-confidence (i.e. in matters of justice) enough to make human intercourse within a society a miserable thing. This riddle holds the key to the wisdom of the world (probably, both the false wisdom of the unenlightened, and the true wisdom of great teachers). This news is old enough, and yet the need for its understanding sees daily proof.

I paraphrase freely, admittedly interpreting difficulties in the light of the recurring philosophy of this play on the blindness of men's moral judgements, and especially in the light of the Duke's personal moral attitude as read from his other words and actions. This speech holds the poetry of ethics. Its content, too, is very close to the Gospel teaching, the insistence on the blindness of the world, its habitual disregard of the truth exposed by prophet and teacher:

> And this is the condemnation, that light is come into the world, and men loved darkness rather than light, because their deeds were evil.
>
> (John, iii. 19)

The same almost divine suggestion rings in many of the Duke's measured prose utterances. There are his supremely beautiful words to Escalus (IV. ii. 219):

> Look, the unfolding star calls up the shepherd. Put not yourself into amazement how these things should be: all difficulties are but easy when they are known.

The first lovely sentence—a unique beauty of Shakespearian prose, in a style peculiar to this play—derives part of its appeal from New Testament associations, and the second sentence holds the mystic assurance of Matthew, x. 26:

> . . . for there is nothing covered, that shall not be revealed; and hid, that shall not be known.

The Duke exercises the authority of a teacher throughout his disguise as a friar. He speaks authoritatively on repentance to Juliet:

> *Duke.* . . . but lest you do repent,
>   As that the sin hath brought you to this shame,
>   Which sorrow is always towards ourselves, not Heaven,
>   Showing we would not spare Heaven as we love it,
>   But as we stand in fear—
> *Juliet.* I do repent me as it is an evil,
>   And take the shame with joy.
> *Duke.* There rest . . .   (II. iii. 30)

After rebuking Pompey the bawd very sternly but not unkindly, he
concludes:

> Go mend, go mend.   (III. ii. 28)

His attitude is that of Jesus to the woman taken in adultery:

> Neither do I condemn thee: go, and sin no more.   (John, viii. 11)

Both are more kindly disposed towards honest impurity than light
and frivolous scandal-mongers, such as Lucio, or Pharisaic self-righteousness such as Angelo's.

The Duke's ethical attitude is exactly correspondent with Jesus':
the play must be read in the light of the Gospel teaching, if its full
significance is to be apparent. So he, like Jesus, moves among men
suffering grief at their sins and deriving joy from an unexpected flower
of simple goodness in the deserts of impurity and hardness. He finds
softness of heart where he least expects it—in the Provost of the
prison:

> *Duke.* This is a gentle provost: seldom when
>   The steeled gaoler is the friend of men. (IV. ii. 89)'

So, too, Jesus finds in the centurion,

> a man under authority, having soldiers under me . . .
>   (Matthew, viii. 9)

a simple faith where he least expects it:

> . . . I say unto you, I have not found so great faith, no, not in Israel.

The two incidents are very similar in quality. Now, in that he represents a perfected ethical philosophy joined to supreme authority, the
Duke is, within the dramatic universe, automatically comparable with
Divinity; or we may suggest that he progresses by successive modes,
from worldly power through the prophecy and moralizing of the middle scenes, to the supreme judgement at the end, where he exactly
reflects the universal judgement as suggested by many Gospel passages.
There is the same apparent injustice, the same tolerance and mercy.
The Duke is, in fact, a symbol of the same kind as the Father in the
Parable of the Prodigal Son (Luke xv) or the Lord in that of the
Unmerciful Servant (Matthew xviii). The simplest way to focus cor-
rectly the quality and unity of *Measure for Measure* is to read it on
the analogy of Jesus' parables.

Though his ethical philosophy is so closely related to the Gospel
teaching, yet the Duke's thoughts on death are devoid of any explicit
belief in immortality. He addresses Claudio, who is to die, and his
words at first appear vague, agnostic: but a deeper acquaintance

renders their profundity and truth. Claudio fears death. The Duke comforts him by concentrating not on death, but on life. In a series of pregnant sentences he asserts the negative nature of any single life-joy. First, life is slave to death and may fail at any chance moment; however much you run from death, yet you cannot but run still towards it; nobility in man is inextricably twined with "baseness" (this is, indeed, the moral of *Measure for Measure*), and courage is ever subject to fear; sleep is man's "best rest," yet he fears death which is but sleep; man is not a single independent unit, he has no solitary self to lose, but rather is compounded of universal "dust"; he is always discontent, striving for what he has not, forgetful of that which he succeeds in winning; man is a changing, wavering substance; his riches he wearily carries till death unloads him; he is tortured by disease and old age. The catalogue is strong in unremittent condemnation of life:

> Thou hast nor youth nor age,
> But, as it were, an after-dinner's sleep,
> Dreaming on both; for all they blessed youth
> Becomes as aged, and doth beg the alms
> Of palsied eld; and when thou art old and rich,
> Thou hast neither heat, affection, limb, nor beauty,
> To make thy riches pleasant. What's yet in this
> That bears the name of life? Yet in this life
> Lie hid moe thousand deaths: yet death we fear,
> That makes these odds all even. (III. i. 32)

Life is therefore a sequence of unrealities, strung together in a time-succession. Everything it can give is in turn killed. Regarded, thus, it is unreal, a delusion, a living death. The thought is profound. True, the Duke has concentrated especially on the temporal aspect of life's appearances, regarding only the shell of life and neglecting the inner vital principle of joy and hope; he has left deeper things untouched. He neglects love and all immediate transcendent intuitions. But since it is only this temporal aspect of decayed appearances which death is known to end, since it is only the closing of this very time-succession which Claudio fears, it is enough to prove this succession valueless. Claudio is thus comforted. The death of such a life is indeed not death, but rather itself a kind of life:

> I humbly thank you.
> To sue to live, I find I seek to die;
> And seeking death, find life: let it come on. (III. i. 41)

Now he "will encounter darkness as a bride," like Antony (III. i. 82). The Duke's death-philosophy is thus the philosophy of the great

tragedies to follow—of *Timon of Athens,* of *Antony and Cleopatra.*
So, too, his ethic is the ethic of *King Lear.* In this problem play we
find the profound thought of the supreme tragedies already emergent
and given careful and exact form, the Duke in this respect being
analogous to Agamemnon in *Troilus and Cressida.* Both his ethical and
his death thinking are profoundly modern. But Claudio soon reverts
to the crude time-thinking (and fine poetry) of his famous death-
speech, in which he regards the after-life in terms of orthodox eschatology, thinking of it as a temporal process, like Hamlet:

> Ay, but to die, and go we know not where . . .   (III. i. 116)

In the Shakespearian mode of progressive thought it is essential first
to feel death's reality strongly as the ender of what we call "life":
only then do we begin to feel the tremendous pressure of an immortality not known in terms of time. We then begin to attach a different
meaning to the words "life" and "death." The thought of this scene
thus wavers between the old and the new death-philosophies.

The Duke's plot pivots on the testing of Angelo. Angelo is a man
of spotless reputation, generally respected. Escalus says

> If any in Vienna be of worth
> To undergo such ample grace and honour,
> It is Lord Angelo.   (I. i. 22)

Angelo, hearing the Duke's praise, and his proposed trust, modestly
declines, as though he recognizes that his virtue is too purely idealistic
for the rough practice of state affairs:

> Now, good my lord,
> Let there be some more test made of my metal,
> Before so noble and so great a figure
> Be stamp'd upon it.   (I. i. 47)

Angelo is not a conscious hypocrite: rather a man whose chief faults
are self-deception and pride in his own righteousness—an unused and
delicate instrument quite useless under the test of active trial. This he
half-recognizes, and would first refuse the proffered honour. The
Duke insists: Angelo's fall is thus entirely the Duke's responsibility.
So this man of ascetic life is forced into authority. He is

> a man whose blood
> Is very snow-broth; one who never feels
> The wanton stings and motions of the sense,
> But doth rebate and blunt his natural edge
> With profits of the mind, study and fast.
>   (I. iv. 57)

Angelo, indeed, does not know himself: no one receives so great a shock as he himself when temptation overthrows his virtue. He is no hypocrite. He cannot, however, be acquitted of Pharisaical pride: his reputation means much to him, he "stands at a guard with envy" (I. iii. 51). He "takes pride" in his "gravity" (II. iv. 10). Now, when he is first faced with the problem of Claudio's guilt of adultery—and commanded, we must presume, by the Duke's sealed orders to execute stern punishment wholesale, for this is the Duke's ostensible purpose —Angelo pursues his course without any sense of wrongdoing. Escalus hints that surely all men must know sexual desire—how then is Angelo's procedure just? Escalus thus adopts the Duke's ethical point of view, exactly:

> Let but your honour know
> (Whom I believe to be most strait in virtue),
> That, in the working of your own affections,
> Had time cohered with place, or place with wishing,
> Or that the resolute acting of your blood
> Could have attain'd the effect of your own purpose,
> Whether you had not, some time in your life,
> Err'd in this point, which now you censure him,
> And pull'd the law upon you. (II. i. 8)

Which reflects the Gospel message:

> Ye have heard that it was said by them of old time, Thou shalt not commit adultery:
> But I say unto you, that whosoever looketh on a woman to lust after her hath committed adultery with her already in his heart.
> (Matthew, v. 27)

Angelo's reply, however, is sound sense:

> 'Tis one thing to be tempted, Escalus,
> Another thing to fall. (II. i. 17)

Isabella later uses the same argument as Escalus:

> . . . Go to your bosom;
> Knock there, and ask your heart what it doth know
> That 's like my brother's fault: if it confess
> A natural guiltiness, such as is his,
> Let it not sound a thought upon your tongue
> Against my brother's life. (II. ii. 136)

We are reminded of Jesus' words to the Scribes and Pharisees concerning the woman "taken in adultery":

He that is without sin among you, let him first cast a stone at her.
                                                          (John, viii. 7)

Angelo is, however, sincere: terribly sincere. He feels no personal responsibility, since he is certain that he does right. We believe him
when he tells Isabella:

> It is the law, not I, condemn your brother:
> Were he my kinsman, brother, or my son,
> It should be thus with him.   (II. ii. 80)

To execute justice, he says, is kindness, not cruelty, in the long run.
Angelo's arguments are rationally conclusive. A thing irrational
breaks them, however: his passion for Isabella. Her purity, her idealism, her sanctity enslave him—she who speaks to him of

> true prayers
> That shall be up at heaven and enter there
> Ere sun-rise, prayers from preserved souls,
> From fasting maids whose minds are dedicate
> To nothing temporal.   (II. ii. 151)

Angelo is swiftly enwrapped in desire. He is finely shown as falling
a prey to his own love of purity and asceticism:

> What is't I dream on?
> O cunning enemy, that, to catch a saint,
> With saints dost bait thy hook!
>   (II. ii. 179)

He "sins in loving virtue"; no strumpet could ever allure him; Isabella
subdues him utterly—now he who built so strongly on a rational
righteousness, understands for the first time the sweet unreason of
love:

> Ever till now,
> When men were fond, I smiled and wonder'd how.
>   (II. ii. 186)

Angelo struggles hard: he prays to Heaven, but his thoughts "anchor"
on Isabel (II. iv. 4). His gravity and learning—all are suddenly as
nothing. He admits to himself that he has taken "pride" in his well-
known austerity: adding "let no man hear me"—a pathetic touch
which casts a revealing light both on his shallow ethic and his honest
desire at this moment to understand himself. The violent struggle is
short. He surrenders—his ideals all toppled over like ninepins:

> Blood, thou art blood:
> Let's write good angel on the Devil's horn,
> 'Tis not the Devil's crest.   (II. iv. 15)

Angelo is now quite adrift: all his old contacts are irrevocably severed. Sexual desire has long been anathema to him, so his warped idealism forbids any healthy love. Good and evil change places in his mind, since this passion is immediately recognized as good, yet, by every one of his stock judgements, condemned as evil. The Devil becomes a "good angel." And this wholesale reversion leaves Angelo in sorry plight now: he has no moral values left. Since sex has been synonymous with foulness in his mind, this new love, reft from the start of moral sanction in a man who "scarce confesses that his blood flows," becomes swiftly a devouring and curbless lust:

> I have begun,
> And now I give my sensual race the rein. (II. iv. 160)

So he addresses Isabella. He imposes the vile condition of Claudio's life. All this is profoundly true: he is at a loss with this new reality—embarrassed as it were, incapable of pursuing a normal course of love. In proportion as his moral reason formerly denied his instincts, so now his instincts assert themselves in utter callousness of his moral reason. He swiftly becomes an utter scoundrel. He threatens to have Claudio tortured. Next, thinking to have had his way with Isabella, he is so conscience-stricken and tortured by fear that he madly resolves not to keep faith with her: he orders Claudio's instant execution. For, in proportion as he is nauseated at his own crimes, he is terror-struck at exposure. He is mad with fear, his story exactly pursues the Macbeth rhythm:

> This deed unshapes me quite, makes me unpregnant
> And dull to all proceedings. A deflower'd maid!
> And by an eminent body that enforced
> The law against it! But that her tender shame
> Will not proclaim against her maiden loss,
> How might she tongue me! Yet reason dares her no;
> For my authority bears so credent bulk,
> That no particular scandal once can touch
> But it confounds the breather. He should have lived,
> Save that his riotous youth, with dangerous sense,
> Might in the times to come have ta'en revenge,
> By so receiving a dishonour'd life
> With ransome of such shame. Would yet he had lived!
> Alack, when once our grace we have forgot,
> Nothing goes right: we would, and we would not.
>   (IV. iv. 23)

This is the reward of self-deception, of pharisaical pride, of an ideal-

ism not harmonized with instinct—of trying, to use the Duke's pregnant phrase:

> To draw with idle spiders' strings
> Most ponderous and substantial things.   (III. ii. 297)

Angelo has not been overcome with evil. He has been ensnared by
good—by his own love of sanctity, exquisitely symbolized in his love
of Isabella: the hook is baited with a saint, and the saint is caught.
The cause of his fall is this and this only. The coin of his moral
purity, which flashed so brilliantly, when tested does not ring true.
Angelo is the symbol of a false intellectualized ethic divorced from
the deeper springs of human instinct.

The varied close-inwoven themes of *Measure for Measure* are finally
knit in the exquisite final act. To that point the action—reflected
image always of the Ducal plot—marches

> By cold gradation and well-balanced form.   (IV. iii. 108)

The last act of judgement is heralded by trumpet calls:

> Twice have the trumpets sounded;
> The generous and gravest citizens
> Have hent the gates, and very near upon
> The Duke is entering.   (IV. vi. 12)

So all are, as it were, summoned to the final judgement. Now Angelo,
Isabella, Lucio—all are understood most clearly in the light of this
scene. The last act is the key to the play's meaning, and all difficulties
are here resolved. I shall observe the judgement measured to each,
noting retrospectively the especial significance in the play of Lucio
and Isabella.

Lucio is a typical loose-minded, vulgar wit. He is the product of a
society that has gone too far in condemnation of human sexual de-
sires. He keeps up a running comment on sexual matters. His very
existence is a condemnation of the society which makes him a possibility. Not that there is anything of premeditated villainy in him:
he is merely superficial, enjoying the unnatural ban on sex which
civilization imposes, because that very ban adds point and spice to
sexual gratification. He is, however, sincerely concerned about Claudio, and urges Isabella to plead for him. He can be serious—for a
while. He can speak sound sense, too, in the full flow of his vulgar wit:

> Yes, in good sooth, the vice is of a great kindred; it is well allied: but
> it is impossible to extirp it quite, friar, till eating and drinking be put

down. They say this Angelo was not made by man and woman after this
downright way of creation: is it true, think you?   (III. ii. 110)

This goes to the root of our problem here. Pompey has voiced the
same thought (II. i. 248–63). This is, indeed, what the Duke has known
too well: what Angelo and Isabella do not know. Thus Pompey and
Lucio here at least tell down-right facts—Angelo and Isabella pursue
impossible and valueless ideals. Only the Duke holds the balance exact
throughout. Lucio's running wit, however, pays no consistent regard
to truth. To him the Duke's leniency was a sign of hidden immorality:

> Ere he would have hanged a man for getting a hundred bastards, he
> would have paid for the nursing of a thousand: he had some feeling of
> the sport; he knew the service, and that instructed him to mercy.
>
> (III. ii. 126)

He traduces the Duke's character wholesale. He does not pause to
consider the truth of his words. Again, there is no intent to harm—
merely a careless, shallow, truthless wit-philosophy which enjoys its
own sex-chatter. The type is common. Lucio is refined and vulgar,
and the more vulgar because of his refinement; whereas Pompey, because of his natural coarseness, is less vulgar. Lucio can only exist in a
society of smug propriety and self-deception: for his mind's life is
entirely parasitical on those insincerities. His false—because fantastic
and shallow—pursuit of sex, is the result of a false, fantastic, denial of
sex in his world. Like so much in *Measure for Measure* he is eminently
modern. Now Lucio is the one person the Duke finds it all but impossible to forgive:

> I find an apt remission in myself;
> And yet here's one in place I cannot pardon. (V. i. 499)

All the rest have been serious in their faults. Lucio's condemnation is
his triviality, his insincerity, his profligate idleness, his thoughtless de-
traction of others' characters:

> You, sirrah, that knew me for a fool, a coward,
> One all of luxury, an ass, a madman;
> Wherein have I so deserved of you,
> That you extol me thus?   (V. i. 501)

Lucio's treatment at the close is eminently, and fittingly, undignified.
He is threatened thus: first he is to marry the mother of his child,
about whose wrong he formerly boasted; then to be whipped and
hanged. Lucio deserves some credit, however: he preserves his nature

and answers with his characteristic wit. He cannot be serious. The
Duke, his sense of humour touched, retracts the sentence:

Duke. Upon mine honour, thou shalt marry her.
  Thy slanders I forgive; and therewithal
  Remit thy other forfeits. Take him to prison;
  And see our pleasure herein executed.
Lucio. Marrying a punk, my lord, is pressing to death, whipping, and
  hanging.
Duke. Slandering a prince deserves it.   (V. i. 520)

Idleness, triviality, thoughtlessness receive the Duke's strongest condemnation. The thought is this:

> But I say unto you, That every idle word that men shall speak, they
> shall give account thereof in the day of judgement. (Matthew xii. 36)

Exactly what happens to Lucio. His wit is often illuminating, often
amusing, sometimes rather disgusting. He is never wicked, is sometimes
almost lovable—but he is terribly dangerous.

    Isabella is the opposite extreme. She is more saintly than Angelo,
and her saintliness goes deeper, is more potent than his. When we first
meet her, she is about to enter the secluded life of a nun. She wel-
comes such a life. She even wishes

> a more strict restraint
> Upon the sisterhood, the votarists of Saint Clare.   (I. iv. 4)

Even Lucio respects her. She calls forth something deeper than his
usual wit:

> I would not—though 'tis my familiar sin
> With maids to seem the lapwing and to jest,
> Tongue far from heart—play with all virgins so:
> I hold you as a thing ensky'd and sainted,
> By your renouncement an immortal spirit,
> And to be talk'd with in sincerity,
> As with a saint.   (I. iv. 31)

Which contains a fine and exact statement of his shallow behaviour,
his habitual wit for wit's sake. Lucio is throughout a loyal friend to
Claudio: truer to his cause, in fact, than Isabella. A pointed contrast.
He urges her to help. She shows a distressing lack of warmth. It is
Lucio that talks of "your poor brother." She is cold:

> *Lucio.*   Assay the power you have.
> *Isabella.* My power? Alas, I doubt—
> *Lucio.*   Our doubts are traitors
> And make us lose the good we oft might win,
> By fearing to attempt.   (I. iv. 76)

Isabella's self-centred saintliness is thrown here into strong contrast with Lucio's manly anxiety for his friend. So, contrasted with Isabella's ice-cold sanctity, there are the beautiful lines with which Lucio introduces the matter to her:

> Your brother and his lover have embraced:
> As those that feed grow full, as blossoming time
> That from the seedness the bare fallow brings
> To teeming foison, even so her plenteous womb
> Expresseth his full tilth and husbandry.

(I. iv. 40)

Compare the pregnant beauty of this with the chastity of Isabella's recent lisping line:

> Upon the sisterhood, the vatarists of Saint Clare.   (I. iv. 5)

Isabella lacks human feeling. She starts her suit to Angelo poorly enough—she is luke-warm:

> There is a vice that most I do abhor,
> And most desire should meet the blow of justice;
> For which I would not plead but that I must;
> For which I must not plead, but that I am
> At war 'twixt will and will not.   (II. ii. 29)

Lucio has to urge her on continually. We begin to feel that Isabella has no real affection for Claudio; has stifled all human love in the pursuit of sanctity. When Angelo at last proposes his dishonourable condition she quickly comes to her decision:

> Then, Isabel, live chaste and, brother, die.
> More than our brother is our chastity.   (II. iv. 185)

When Shakespeare chooses to load his dice like this—which is seldom indeed—he does it mercilessly. The Shakespearian satire here strikes once, and deep: there is no need to point it further. But now we know our Isabel. We are not surprised that she behaves to Claudio, who hints for her sacrifice, like a fiend:

> Take my defiance!
> Die, perish! Might but my bending down
> Reprieve thee from thy fate, it should proceed:
> I'll pray a thousand prayers for thy death,
> No word to save thee.   (III. i. 141)

Is her fall any less than Angelo's? Deeper, I think. With whom is Isabel angry? Not only with her brother. She has feared this choice—

terribly: "O, I do fear thee, Claudio," she said (III. i. 72). Even since
Angelo's suggestion she has been afraid. Now Claudio has forced the
responsibility of choice on her. She cannot sacrifice herself. Her sex
inhibitions have been horribly shown her as they are, naked. She has
been stung—lanced on a sore spot of her soul. She knows now that
it is not all saintliness, she sees her own soul and sees it as something
small, frightened, despicable, too frail to dream of such a sacrifice.
Though she does not admit it, she is infuriated not with Claudio,
but with herself. "Saints" should not speak like this. Again, the comment of this play is terribly illuminating. It is significant that she
readily involves Mariana in illicit love: it is always her own, and only
her own, chastity that assumes, in her heart, universal importance.

Isabella, however, was no hypocrite, any more than Angelo. She is
a spirit of purity, grace, maiden charm: but all these virtues the
action of the play turns remorselessly against herself. In a way, it is
not her fault. Chastity is hardly a sin—but neither, as the play emphasizes, is it the whole of virtue. And she, like the rest, has to find
a new wisdom. Mariana in the last act prays for Angelo's life. Confronted by that warm, potent, forgiving, human love, Isabella herself
suddenly shows a softening, a sweet humanity. Asked to intercede, she
does so—she, who was at the start slow to intercede for a brother's
life, now implores the Duke to save Angelo, her wronger:

> I partly think
> A due sincerity govern'd his deeds,
> Till he did look on me.
>
> (V. i. 446)

There is a suggestion that Angelo's strong passion has itself moved
her, thawing her ice-cold pride. This is the moment of her trial: the
Duke is watching her keenly, to see if she has learnt her lesson—nor
does he give her any help, but deliberately puts obstacles in her way.
But she stands the test: she bows to a love greater than her own saintliness. Isabella, like Angelo, has progressed far during the play's action:
from sanctity to humanity.

Angelo, at the beginning of this final scene, remains firm in denial
of the accusations levelled against him. Not till the Duke's disguise as
a friar is made known and he understands that deception is no longer
possible, does he show outward repentance. We know, however, that
his inward thoughts must have been terrible enough—his earlier
agonized soliloquies put this beyond doubt. Now, his failings exposed,
he seems to welcome punishment:

> Immediate sentence then and sequent death
> Is all the grace I beg.   (V. i. 374)

Escalus expresses sorrow and surprise at his actions. He answers:

> I am sorry that such sorrow I procure:
> And so deep sticks it in my penitent heart
> That I crave death more willingly than mercy;
> 'Tis my deserving and I do entreat it.
>   (V. i. 475)

To Angelo, exposure seems to come as a relief: the horror of self-deception is at an end. For the first time in his life he is both quite honest with himself and with the world. So he takes Mariana as his wife. This is just: he threw her over because he thought she was not good enough for him,

> Partly for that her promised proportions
> Came short of composition, but in chief
> For that her reputation was disvalued
> In levity.   (V. i. 213)

He aimed too high when he cast his eyes on the sainted Isabel: now, knowing himself, he will find his true level in the love of Mariana. He has become human. The union is symbolical. Just as his supposed love-contact with Isabel was a delusion, when Mariana, his true mate, was taking her place, so Angelo throughout has deluded himself. Now his acceptance of Mariana symbolizes his new self-knowledge. So, too, Lucio is to find his proper level in marrying Mistress Kate Keepdown, of whose child he is the father. Horrified as he is at the thought, he has to meet the responsibilities of his profligate behaviour. The punishment of both is this only: to know, and to be, themselves. This is both their punishment and at the same time their highest reward for their sufferings: self-knowledge being the supreme, perhaps the only, good. We remember the parable of the Pharisee and the Publican (Luke xviii).

So the Duke draws his plan to its appointed end. All, including Barnadine, are forgiven, and left, in the usual sense, unpunished. This is inevitable. The Duke's original leniency has been shown by his successful plot to have been right, not wrong. Though he sees "corruption boil and bubble" (V. i. 316) in Vienna, he has found, too, that man's sainted virtue is a delusion: "judge not that ye be not judged." He has seen an Angelo to fall from grace at the first breath of power's temptation, he has seen Isabella's purity scarring, defacing her humanity. He has found more gentleness in "the steeled gaoler" than in either of these. He has found more natural honesty in Pompey the bawd than in Angelo the ascetic; more humanity in the charity of Mistress Overdone than in Isabella condemning her brother to death with venomed words in order to preserve her own chastity. Mistress Overdone has looked after Lucio's illegitimate child:

> . . . Mistress Kate Keepdown was with child by him in the Duke's time; he promised her marriage; his child is a year and a quarter old, come Philip and Jacob: I have kept it myself . . .   (III. ii. 215)

Human virtue does not flower only in high places: nor is it the monopoly of the pure in body. In reading *Measure for Measure* one feels that Pompey with his rough humour and honest professional indecency is the only one of the major persons, save the Duke, who can be called "pure in heart." Therefore, knowing all this, the Duke knows his tolerance to be now a moral imperative: he sees too far into the nature of man to pronounce judgement according to the appearances of human behaviour. But we are not told what will become of Vienna. There is, however, a hint, for the Duke is to marry Isabel, and this marriage, like the others, may be understood symbolically. It is to be the marriage of understanding with purity; of tolerance with moral fervour. The Duke, who alone has no delusions as to the virtues of man, who is incapable of executing justice on vice since he finds forgiveness implicit in his wide and sympathetic understanding—he alone wins the "enskied and sainted" Isabel—more, we are not told. And we may expect her in future to learn from him wisdom, human tenderness, and love:

> What's mine is yours and what is yours is mine.
> (V. i. 539)

If we still find this universal forgiveness strange—and many have done so— we might observe Mariana, who loves Angelo with a warm and realistically human love. She sees no fault in him, or none of any consequence:

> O my dear lord,
> I crave no other nor no better man.
> (V. i. 426)

She knows that

> best men are moulded out of faults,
> And, for the most, become much more the better
> For being a little bad.
>
> (V. i. 440)

The incident is profoundly true. Love asks no questions, sees no evil, transfiguring the just and unjust alike. This is one of the surest and finest ethical touches in this masterpiece of ethical drama. Its moral of love is, too, the ultimate splendour of Jesus' teaching.

Measure for Measure is indeed based firmly on that teaching. The lesson of the play is that of Matthew, v. 20:

> For I say unto you, That except your righteousness shall exceed the righteousness of the scribes and Pharisees, ye shall in no case enter into the Kingdom of Heaven.

The play must be read, not as a picture of normal human affairs, but as a parable, like the parables of Jesus. The plot is, in fact, an inversion of one of those parables—that of the Unmerciful Servant (Matthew, xviii); and the universal and level forgiveness at the end, where all alike meet pardon, is one with the forgiveness of the Parable of the Two Debtors (Luke, vii). Much has been said about the difficulties of *Measure for Measure*. But, in truth, no play of Shakespeare shows more thoughtful care, more deliberate purpose, more consummate skill in structural technique, and, finally, more penetrating ethical and psychological insight. None shows a more exquisitely inwoven pattern. And, if ever the thought at first sight seems strange, or the action unreasonable, it will be found to reflect the sublime strangeness and unreason of Jesus' teaching.

The Renaissance Background of
Measure for Measure

by Elizabeth Marie Pope

When critics of *Measure for Measure*[1] are not staggered or repelled by the ethical presuppositions upon which the characters act, they usually try to justify and explain the work on the ground that its morality is specifically Christian. But while such scholars as Roy Battenhouse, C. J. Sisson and R. W. Chambers have thus defended Shakespeare's treatment of law, authority, justice, and mercy, they have not inquired what exact meaning was attached to these terms in the Renaissance, apparently because they assume that he thought of them very much as we do.[2] But did he? What doctrines of equity and forgiveness were actually taught to the Elizabethan layman? Would the first audience that saw *Measure for Measure* find them in the play? Can they explain anything in Shakespeare's presentation of the subject that we might otherwise overlook or misunderstand? And for the answers to these questions we must turn to the popular religious text-books of Shakespeare's own day—not to the Church Fathers or the Latin works of the great contemporary Reformers and Counter-Reformers, but to the annotated Bibles, the translations, the English commentaries, the sermons, and the tracts through which the teaching of the Church reached the individual without special training or interest in theology.

"*The Renaissance Background of* Measure for Measure" *by Elizabeth Marie Pope. From* Shakespeare Survey, *II (Cambridge University Press, 1949), 66–82. Reprinted by permission of Cambridge University Press and the author.*

[1] This article is based on material gathered when the writer was holder of a research fellowship at the Folger Shakespeare Library.

[2] R. W. Battenhouse, "*Measure for Measure* and Christian Doctrine of the Atonement," *P.M.L.A.* LXI (1946), 1029–59; C. J. Sisson, *The Mythical Sorrows of Shakespeare* (Annual Shakespeare Lecture of the British Academy, 1934), p. 17; R. W. Chambers, *The Jacobean Shakespeare and "Measure for Measure"* (Annual Shakespeare Lecture of the British Academy, 1937), p. 54. [An excerpt from the revision of Chambers' lecture is published in this book—ED.]

The first point to be noted is that *Measure for Measure,* unlike some of Shakespeare's comedies, has a highly significant title, a phrase which not only sums up the basic theme of the play, but is brought out and emphasized at the crisis in the last act, when the Duke condemns his deputy:

> "An Angelo for Claudio, death for death."
> Haste still pays haste, and leisure answers leisure;
> Like doth quit like, and Measure still for Measure.
>   (V. i. 414–6)

Shakespeare is of course thinking of a verse from the Sermon on the Mount: "With what measure ye mete it shall be measured to you again." In both Matthew and Luke, however, the text is not isolated, but forms an integral part of a short passage which in Luke immediately follows—and is linked with—Christ's great pronouncement on Christian forgiveness:

27 . . . Love your enemies: do well to them which hate you. . . .

31 And as ye would that men should do to you, so do ye to them likewise.

32 For if ye love them which love you, what thank shall ye have: for even the sinners love those that love them. [The Matthew, Bishops, and Great Bibles read: "for sinners also love their lovers."]

33 And if ye do good for them which do good for you, what thank shall ye have? for even the sinners do the same. . . .

35 Wherefore love ye your enemies, and do good, and lend, looking for nothing again, and your reward shall be great, and ye shall be the children of the most High: for he is kind unto the unkind, and to the evil.

36 Be ye therefore merciful, as your Father also is merciful.

37 Judge not, and ye shall not be judged: condemn not, and ye shall not be condemned: forgive, and ye shall be forgiven.

38 Give, and it shall be given unto you: a good measure, pressed down, shaken together, and running over shall men give into your bosom: for with what measure ye mete, with the same shall men mete to you again.

39 And he spake a parable unto them, Can the blind lead the blind? Shall they not both fall into the ditch?

40 The disciple is not above his master: but whosoever will be a perfect disciple, shall be as his master.

41 And why seest thou a mote in thy brother's eye, and considerest not the beam that is in thine own eye?

42 Either how canst thou say to thy brother, Brother, let me pull out the mote that is in thine eye, when thou seest not the beam that is in thine own eye? Hypocrite, cast the beam out of thine own eye

first, and then shalt thou see perfectly to pull out the mote that is in thy brother's eye.[3]

Matt. vii, 1–5 corresponds to Luke vi, 36–42, but does not include verses 36, 39 or 40, and does not follow or refer to the command to forgive. Luke vi, 36–42 was evidently considered the more authoritative rendering of the passage: it was the one chosen by the Anglican Church as the gospel for the fourth Sunday after Trinity; as such, it was also the one analysed in the postils (or formal collections of sermons on the assigned readings for the year); and the most famous and popular of the annotated Bibles, the Geneva version, assigns it five explanatory notes as against one to the equivalent texts in Matthew. Doctrinal teaching on the Luke passage, however, differs only slightly from that on the Matthew; and it is this teaching which is of primary importance, since it covers most—if not all—of the major ethical issues that appear in *Measure for Measure*.

To begin with, the authorities argue, the passage shows that it is intolerable when a man "narrowly examineth his brother's manners, and is desirous to bewray his brother's fault," especially if at the same time he neither recognizes nor regrets his own.[4] Critics who are themselves vicious can no more correct others than the blind can lead the blind. The little allegory of the mote and the beam is meant to drive home and reinforce the same lesson. "O how uncomely," cries the author of the *Brief Postil,*

> how wicked, how hypocrite like, how uncharitable a thing it is, to judge our neighbours of light matters, whereas we be an hundred time worse ourselves! Why do we not rather gently bear, dissemble, and interpret well the small error and fault of our brethren? Why do we

[3] Luke vi, 27–42. Geneva version (London, 1599). The spelling of this and all subsequent citations from Renaissance sources has been modernized for the convenience of the reader.

[4] John Calvin, quoted by Augustine Marlorate, in his *Catholike and Ecclesiasticall Exposition of . . . S. Mathewe*, trans. Thomas Tymme (London, 1570), p. 136. See also J. Calvin, *A Harmonie vpon . . . Matthewe, Marke, and Luke*, trans. E. P. (London, 1584), p. 209; *The Epistles and Gospelles with a Brief Postil* [ed. R. Taverner], (n.p., 1540), sig. Bb. 1r; Desiderius Erasmus, *The First Tome . . . of the Paraphrase . . . vpon the Newe Testament* (London, 1548), fol. lxxvii^v; [Antonius Corvinus], *A Postill . . . vpon Euery Gospell through the Yeare* (n.p., 1550), sigs. Pii^v–Piiii^v; Nicholas Heminge [Niel Hemmingsen]. *A Postill or Exposition of the Gospels*, trans. Arthur Golding (London, 1569), fol. 208^r; William Perkins, *Exposition of Christs Sermon in the Mount* (Cambridge, 1608), pp. 408–13; the Rheims note on Matt. vii, 1 in William Fulke's *Text of the Newe Testament . . . translated out of the vulgar Latine by the Papists of the Traiterous Seminarie at Rhemes* (London, 1589), sig. Fiv.

not rather go down to the entrails of our own heart, and see our own stuff? [5]

The forbearance recommended must not of course be carried to the point of condoning or refusing to censure open and serious wrong. As Calvin puts it:

> He which judgeth by the rule of charity, always first examining himself, he, I say, keepeth the true and right order of judging. Nevertheless it is not only lawful for us to condemn all sins, but also it is necessary, except we will abrogate the laws of God and overthrow his judgement. For he would have us to be proclaimers of his sentences which he pronounceth as concerning the deeds of men.[6]

William Perkins, in his *Treatise of Christian Equity and Moderation* (Cambridge, 1604), is even more emphatic: courtesy and tolerance, he insists, are proper only so long as

> they whom we forbear . . . do not exceed, nor break out into any outrage, or extremity: for then they are not to be forborne, but to be told, and reproved for them, and man's duty is not to wink at them, but to take notice of them, and to show open dislike of them [p. 41].

But otherwise we are strictly forbidden to judge, condemn, or refuse to forgive our fellows. In the first place, we ought to be merciful, even as God also is merciful:

> Because that he hath pardoned and forgiven all our offences and trespasses, of his mere grace, without any deserving, and that through his only son Jesus Christ . . . according to this example, our heavenly father requireth the same thing of us.[7]

This argument is, as one might expect, used chiefly by writers on Luke, who so pointedly links his version of the passage with the doctrine of Christian forgiveness. Secondly—and on this tenet all the authorities agree—we ought to remember that whatever we do invites retaliation in kind. The good will receive their own back with interest, and "so in like manner," says Martin Bucer,

[5] *Brief Postil*, sig. Bb. 1ʳ. See also Calvin, p. 211; Musculus and Bullinger, quoted by Marlorate, *Exposition of Matthew*, p. 137; Thomas Becon, *A New Postil* (London, 1566), sigs. Eeiʳ–Eeiiᵛ; note on Luke vi, 42 in Geneva Bible; Perkins, *Exposition*, pp. 419–31; Corvinus, sig. Piiiiᵛ; Erasmus, fol. lxxviiiʳ; Heminge, fol. 210ᵛ.

[6] Calvin, p. 209. See also Marlorate, *Exposition of Matthew*, p. 136; *Brief Postil*, sig. Bb. 1ʳ; Rheims note on Matt. vii, 1; Geneva note on Luke vi, 37; Perkins, *Exposition*, pp. 408, 424–5; Erasmus, fol. lxxviiᵛ.

[7] Corvinus, sig. Piiiiᵛ. See also Becon, sigs. Ddiʳ–Ddiiiʳ; Ddvʳ–Ddviʳ; *Brief Postil*, sigs. Aa. iijʳ–Aa. iijᵛ; Erasmus, fol. lxxviiʳ; Heminge, fols. 208ᵛ and 209ᵛ.

they which are malicious against others, seekers of revengement, mindful
of wrongs past, straight examiners and judgers of other men's faults,
shall find also, by God's justice, such as shall handle them after the
like fashion.[8]

The continual use of the passive voice in the Gospels—"ye shall be
judged," "ye shall be condemned"—makes it uncertain just who is to
exact this reckoning. Becon and Corvinus assume that it is God, but
the general consensus seems to be rather that it is other men, for, as
Calvin explains, "though this be done by the just vengeance of God,
that they should again be punished, which have judged others: yet the
Lord doth execute this punishment by men" (p. 210). To back this
hypothesis, there is the fact that in Luke (though not in Matthew),
Christ declares that "a good measure . . . shall *men* give into your
bosom"; and we must also remember that according to the four
English translations most widely used in the sixteenth century—the
Matthew, the Great Bible, the Geneva, and the Bishops—the sentence
immediately following ought to read: "For with what measure ye
mete, with the same shall *men* mete to you again." Here or elsewhere
Shakespeare evidently picked up the idea that the verse was to be
taken in this sense: Richard of Gloucester uses it in *3 Henry VI* to
justify the most savage and literal sort of retaliation in kind:

> From off the gates of York fetch down the head,
> Your father's head, which Clifford placed there;
> Instead whereof let this supply the room.
> Measure for measure must be answered.
>
> (II. vi. 52–5)

But however natural and authorized such an interpretation of the
text might have been, it was not quite a satisfactory one when the
passage was considered as a whole, especially in the Luke version.
For who actually is to return rash judgment for rash judgment, condemnation for condemnation, like for like? Men? The same men who
have just been explicitly commanded to forbear judgment and forgive
injuries?[9] God, then? The same God whom His Son has just described as "kind to the unkind, and to the evil," the Father according
to Whose example we are urged to be merciful? At least one Renais-

---

[8] Quoted by Marlorate in *A Catholike and Ecclesiastical Exposition of . . .
S. Mark and S. Luke,* trans. Thomas Tymme (London, 1583), p. 160. See also
Calvin, pp. 209–10; Perkins, *Exposition,* p. 415; *Brief Postil,* sig. Aa. iv^v; Corvinus,
sigs. Pv^r–Pv^v; Becon, sig. Eei^r; Erasmus, fol. lxxvii^v; Heminge, fol. 210^r.

[9] It should also be noted that in Matt. v, 38 ff., the passage which corresponds
to the pronouncement on Christian forgiveness in Luke (vi, 27–35) begins with
a specific repudiation of the *lex talionis.*

sance theologian, William Perkins, seems to have been so distressed by these alternatives that he feels obliged to explain in his *Exposition* (p. 417) that though God does not will men to return evil for evil, and those who indulge in the practice are miserable sinners, God nevertheless uses their wickedness to punish the other miserable sinners who have done evil in the first place. But the rest of the commentators I have seen hardly appear to recognize the problem at all. It is almost as if they approve of mercy at one level of consciousness, and of retaliation in kind at another: separate concepts which do not interact and remain essentially unfused, like the responsibilities Pooh-Bah attaches to his various offices in *The Mikado*. One is certainly aware of a logical incoherence, a failure to think through the question clearly or completely. We may of course argue that if the professional exponents of the Scriptures did not perceive these difficulties, they would scarcely be likely to worry the Elizabethan layman; but it is at least conceivable that a sensitive reader of the passage, even in the sixteenth century, might have observed them—and been troubled.

One more point of doctrine still remains to be discussed. Since extreme sects like the Anabaptists habitually used Scriptural authority to support their arguments for a community of goods, the abolition of civil government, and the like, Protestant theologians took particular pains to qualify or explain away texts capable of any such dangerous interpretation; and as a result we find Becon, Corvinus, Heminge, Perkins, and the author of the *Brief Postil* going out of their way to make it clear that the commands to be merciful, to forgive, and to abstain from judging are meant to bind only the private individual, not to restrict or abolish the authority of the State. Even the Geneva Bible devotes part of its limited and precious marginal space to a note on Luke, vi, 37, warning the reader that Christ "speaketh not here of civil judgments, and therefore by the words, forgive, is meant that good nature which the Christians use in suffering and pardoning wrongs." "Mark, my friends," says the author of the *Brief Postil,*

> that this is only spoken of private judgment and private condemnation, that is to say, I may not be mine own judge, I may not revenge mine own quarrel. . . . It is lawful for rulers, to judge and to condemn, because they do it not in their own name, but as God's ministers and vicars. To this do all the ancient expositors and doctors agree, as Saint Austin, Jerome, Ambrose, Chrysostom, and the rest. Wherefore the wicked Anabaptists are to be banished which condemn temporal or civil judgments.[10]

On the other hand, the civil magistrate was evidently not considered

---

[10] *Brief Postil*, sigs. Aa. iij^v–Aa. iv^r. See also Becon, sigs. Ddiii^r–Ddiii^v; Corvinus, sig. Piiii^r; Heminge, fols. 207^v, 208^r, 209^r; Perkins, *Exposition*, pp. 407–8.

entirely exempt from all the rules Christ lays down in this passage, especially the stipulation that a man should not try to pull the mote from his brother's eye before casting the beam out of his own. "Consider," writes William Perkins in his *Exposition,*

> how Christ would have all those which are to give judgment of the offences of others to be themselves without reproof or blame: else they are no fit persons to give censure of those that be under them. And therefore the Magistrate in the town and commonwealth . . . and every superior in his place must labour to be unblameable [p. 424].

But when the theologians begin arguing in this vein, they are drawing into the discussion the whole question of the rights and obligations of the temporal authority; and it is to the special studies made of this particular subject that we must turn for further light on our problem.

Sermons and treatises defining the status, privileges, and responsibilities of the Christian governor are plentiful enough during the sixteenth century—Antony Guevara's *Dial of Princes,* translated by North in 1557; Geoffrey Fenton's *Forme of Christian Pollicie* (1574); Henry Bullinger's *Fiftie Godlie and Learned Sermons* (1587); James I's *Basilicon Doron* (1599), to name only a few. But in 1603 and 1604, public interest in the question seems to have been especially keen. In those years, King James's *True Lawe of Free Monarchies* was reprinted twice and his *Basilicon Doron* seven times—nine if we count the Welsh translation and William Willymat's digest in Latin and English verse. There also appeared a number of works dealing wholly or in part with the office and duties of the Christian ruler—such as six sermons preached before King James at various times by Thomas Bilson, Richard Eedes, Henry Hooke, Thomas Blague, and Richard Field; reprints of Henry Smith's *Magistrates Scripture* and *Memento for Magistrates;* Andrew Willet's *Ecclesia Triumphans,* a tract showing how James met all the requirements of an ideal ruler; *A Loyal Subiect's Looking-Glasse,* by William Willymat; Ben Jonson's *Panegyre* on the King's first entrance into Parliament; and William Perkins' posthumous *Treatise of Christian Equity and Moderation.* This outburst of concern with the theory of government seems to have been inspired primarily by the accession of James. A certain amount of such preaching and writing would probably have occurred on the arrival of any new monarch, but in this particular case, it must have been greatly stimulated by the fact that the new monarch was himself an authority on the subject, whose work was being eagerly discussed by the public and whose favour the court clergy and *literati* were naturally anxious to gain. It is noticeable how much of the material listed above was originally composed to be delivered before James himself, and how many of the authors manage to include flattering tributes to their royal master and his work in the field, as Thomas Bilson did:

> In the Prince's duty I may be shorter, because I speak before a religious and learned King, who both by pen and practice hath witnessed to the world these many years, how well acquainted he is with Christian and godly government.[11]

Now *Measure for Measure* is very largely concerned with the "Prince's duty," particularly in regard to the administration of justice. At no time, perhaps, could Shakespeare have presented such a subject without reckoning to some extent on what his audience would be predisposed to think of his characters and their behaviour. But if he *did* write the play about 1603–4, he had unusually good reason to believe the subject would be popular and to consider it in terms of the contemporary doctrine of rule—even if we do not assume that he, like so many others, was seriously concerned over the problems of Christian and godly government and deliberately trying to catch the eye of the King, at whose court it was acted and to whose well-known dislike of crowds two passages apparently allude (I. i. 67–73; II. iv. 26–9).

According to Renaissance theory, the authority of all civil rulers is derived from God. Hence, they may be called "gods," as they are in Psalm lxxxii, 6, because they act as God's substitutes, "Ruling, Judging, and Punishing in God's stead, and so deserving God's name here on earth," as Bilson put it in the sermon he preached at King James's coronation.[12] "The Prince," says Henry Smith in his *Magistrates Scripture* (pp. 339–40), "is like a great Image of God, the Magistrates are like little Images of God," though he is careful to

---

[11] Thomas Bilson, *A Sermon Preached at Westminister before the King and Queenes Maiesties, at their Coronations* (London, 1603), sigs. C3ʳ–C3ᵛ. See also Andrew Willet, *Ecclesia Triumphans* [1603], (Cambridge, 1614), p. 33 and sigs. A3ʳ–A4ʳ, A4ᵛ–A5ʳ; William Willymat, *A Loyal Subiects Looking-Glasse* (London, [1604]), sig. A1ʳ, pp. 10, 39, 46; Richard Eedes, "The Dutie of a King," two sermons preached before James (9 and 30 August, 1603), printed in *Six Learned and Godly Sermons* (London, 1604), sigs. Fijᵛ–Fiijʳ.

[12] Bilson, sigs. A6ᵛ–A7ᵛ. See also Perkins, *Treatise*, p. 6; Willymat, pp. 3–4, 5–6; Willet, p. 3; Richard Field, *A Learned Sermon Preached Before the King* (London, 1604), sigs. A3ᵛ–A4ʳ; Henry Smith, *The Magistrates Scripture* [1590], printed in *Sermons* (London, 1631), p. 344; Ben Jonson, *King James His Royall and Magnificent Entertainment* (London, 1604), sig. A4ᵛ; Erasmus Sarcerius, *Commonplaces of Scripture*, trans. R. Taverner (n.p., 1538), fol. lxxi; H. Bullinger, *Fiftie Godlie and Learned Sermons*, trans. H. I. (London, 1587), pp. 152, 219; Geoffrey Fenton, *A Forme of Christian Pollicie* (London, 1574), p. 61; G. Gifford, *A Dialogue Betweene a Papist and Protestant* (London, 1599), pp. 101–2; James I, *True Lawe of Free Monarchies* (London, 1604), sig. B3ʳ.

point out that they are not indeed divine: the name is given them
only to remind them that they are appointed by the Lord "to rule as
he would rule, judge as he would judge, correct as he would correct,
reward as he would reward." This doctrine may very well explain
why the Duke moves through so much of the action of *Measure for
Measure* like an embodied Providence; why his character has such
curiously allegorical overtones, yet never quite slips over the edge into
actual allegory; and finally, why Roy Battenhouse's theory that Shakespeare subconsciously thought of him as the Incarnate Lord is at
once so convincing and so unsatisfactory. Any Renaissance audience
would have taken it for granted that the Duke did indeed "stand for"
God, but only as any good ruler "stood for" Him; and if he behaved
"like power divine," it was because that was the way a good ruler
was expected to conduct himself.

Furthermore, since the ruler's authority was considered an exten-
sion of the same kind of power God delegates to parents, teachers,
ministers, masters, shepherds, and husbands, all these terms were frequently used to describe him, especially "father" and "shepherd." [13]
So when the Duke compares himself to a fond father who has not
disciplined his children for so long that they have run wild (I. iii. 23–
8), the image probably meant rather more to a Renaissance audience
than it would mean to a modern one. When later, after his discussion
with the Provost, he rises at dawn to go about his work with the
remark: "Look, th'unfolding star calls up the shepherd" (IV. ii. 219),
one wonders if he may not be thinking of himself and his office. God
was, moreover, supposed to endow rulers with what was called "suffi-
ciency of spirit" to carry out their duties, though He might withdraw
this gift if they disobeyed Him, as He withdrew it from Saul.[14] It is
possible that this doctrine has some bearing on the treatment of Angelo
in *Measure for Measure,* though there is no reason why Shakespeare
should not have been thinking of something much more elementary

---

[13] The reason for applying such terms to rulers is given by Bilson, sigs. B5^r–B5^v,
C3^r; [*Homilies*] *Certaine Sermons Appointed by the Queens Maiestie* (London,
1595), sig. 13^r; Bullinger, pp. 145–6; J. Dod and R. Cleaver, *Exposition of the Ten
Commandments* (London, 1604), p. 181; R. Bellarmine, *An Ample Declaration of
the Christian Doctrine* (Roane, n.d.), p. 182; Henry Smith, *A Memento for Magis-
trates,* printed in *Sermons* (London, 1604), pp. 534–5. The ruler is also called, or
compared to, a "parent," or "shepherd," or "teacher," etc. by Willet, sig. A2^r;
Jonson, *Panegyre,* in *Entertainment,* sig. F1^r; Fenton, p. 310; Antony Guevara, *The
Dial of Princes,* trans. T. North (n.p., 1568), 1, 53^v; Laurentius Grimaldus Goslicius,
The Counsellor, trans. anon. (London, 1598), p. 74; James I, *True Lawe,* sigs. B4^r,
B4^v–B5^r, D2^v–D3^v, and *Basilicon Doron* (London, 1603), p. 25. See also commentaries
on measure-for-measure passage: Becon, sig. Ddiii^r; Perkins, *Exposition,* p. 424.

[14] Bilson, sigs. A7^v–A8^r; Eedes, sigs. Ev^v–Evi^r; Smith, *Magistrates Scripture,* pp.
341–3, 337, and *Memento for Magistrates,* p. 530.

when he showed him failing to pray successfully after his fall, or lamenting:

> Alack, when once our grace we have forgot,
> Nothing goes right—we would, and we would not.
>
> (IV. iv. 31-2)

In their capacity as God's substitutes, rulers have four privileges. The first is sanctity of person, especially in the case of an anointed prince. No man may raise his hand against him, or even disparage him in speech or thought.[15] To abuse a ruler, according to William Willymat, by "evil speaking, mocking, scorning, scoffing, deriding, reviling, cursing," is a thing "most unhonourable, yea worthy of death" (p. 32)—a belief which must have made Lucio's malicious gossip about the Duke appear a much more serious offence than it seems to a modern audience. Secondly, the ruler has sovereignty of power: all men must obey him without question, except when his commands directly contradict God's ordinances. Even then, disobedience must be entirely passive, and any retaliation from the authorities endured with patience—although Roman Catholics held that open rebellion was sometimes permissible when the ruler was a heretic.[16] As the authorities in *Measure for Measure* are not heretics, this particular question does not arise: there is no doubt that the characters are legally bound to reverence and obey them. But this raised a problem which required—and received—very delicate handling. Since to yield to Angelo would mean breaking a law of God, Isabella is fully entitled to resist him; but the measures taken to circumvent him are by no means passive and might even have been considered to savour dangerously of conspiracy against a lawful magistrate if Shakespeare did not slip neatly away from the whole difficulty by making the chief conspirator the highest officer of the State himself. And as if to ensure that no one should miss the point, he brings it out clearly and carefully in IV. ii, where the excellent Provost refuses to join the plot to save Claudio until he is convinced by the Duke's letter that the friar has the necessary secular power to override the deputy.

The third privilege of rulers is the right to enforce the law. In civil matters, the avenging of evil, which God has strictly forbidden to private individuals, is the office and duty of the ruler and his

---

[15] Bilson, sigs. B1ʳ–B1ᵛ; *Homilies,* sigs. I8ᵛ–K2ʳ; Mm4ᵛ–Nn1ᵛ; Nn7ʳ–Nn7ᵛ; Bullinger, p. 219; Dod and Cleaver, pp. 235-6.

[16] Bilson, sigs. B6ʳ–B6ᵛ; Willymat, pp. 4-5, 26-7, 44-5; *Homilies,* sigs. I5ᵛ–I8ᵛ; Bullinger, pp. 173-5; Dod and Cleaver, p. 236; Nicholas Gibbens, *Questions and Disputations Concerning the Holy Scriptures* (n.p., 1601), p. 377; James I, *True Lawe,* sigs. B7ᵛ–C5ᵛ ff; Gifford, pp. 145-51.

subordinates,[17] to whom the Duke bids Isabella turn when, in her agony at Claudio's supposed death, she momentarily thinks of punishing Angelo herself. The further question of the ruler's title to authority in ecclesiastical as well as civil matters (since, as King James puts it in the *Basilicon Doron,* p. 110, "a King is not *mere laicus,* as both the Papists and Anabaptists would have him; to the which error the Puritans also incline over-far") is not brought up in *Measure for Measure.*

Finally, the ruler has the privilege of using extraordinary means. As Gentillet points out, this certainly does not imply that he is entitled to deceive, betray, and commit perjury in the manner recommended by Machiavelli, but only, in the words of William Willymat, that

> Kings, Princes, and governors do use oftentimes to use diverse causes to disguise their purposes with pretences and colours of other matters, so that the end of their drifts and secret purposes are not right seen into nor understood at the first, this to be lawful the word of God doth not deny.

He then cites the examples of Solomon ordering the child divided; Jehu pretending he would serve Baal, when by this subtlety he really intended to destroy the servants of Baal (II Kings x); and the Emperor Constantius threatening to persecute the Christians when all he actually meant to do was by this stratagem to separate the sheep from the goats.[18] Hence, the Duke in *Measure for Measure* is quite justified in using disguise, applying "craft against vice" (III. ii. 291), and secretly watching Angelo much as King James advises his son in the *Basilicon Doron* to watch his own subordinates: "Delight to haunt your Session, and spy carefully their proceedings . . . to take a sharp account of every man in his office" (pp. 90–2). There would have been no need to apologize for these practices to a Renaissance audience; they would have shrugged them off with the equivalent of Willymat's conclusion to his argument: "Had it not been great lack of wisdom to have interrupted these Christian princes' pretences

---

[17] Bilson, sigs. B3ᵛ–B4ᵛ; Perkins, *Treatise,* pp. 6–7; *Two Guides to a Good Life* (London, 1604), sig. G2ᵛ; Willymat, pp. 48–9; Sarcerius, fols. lxxiiᵛ, ccvʳ, ccviiiʳ; Innocent Gentillet, *A Discovrse vpon the Meanes of Wel Governing,* trans. Simon Patericke (London, 1602), pp. 109–10; *Homilies,* sigs. F2ᵛ–F3ᵛ, I4ʳ–I5ᵛ; Bullinger, pp. 168, 196–8; Fenton, pp. 75–6; Gibbens, pp. 376–7; Bellarmine, pp. 153–4; James I, *True Lawe,* sigs. D5ᵛ–D6ʳ. See also commentaries on the measure-for-measure passage: listed under note 10, above.

[18] Willymat, pp. 58–9. For other arguments in favour of the ruler's right to use extraordinary means, see Bilson, sig. B4ᵛ; Gentillet, pp. 246–51; Goslicius, pp. 90, 119–20; James I, *True Lawe,* sigs. Diᵛ–D2ʳ.

and commandments tending as afterward proved to so good an end?"

But in the eyes of the Renaissance, the Christian prince had not only authority and privileges, but a clearly defined and inescapable set of duties to perform as well. The first is to remember that he is not really God, but man "dressed in a little brief authority," as Isabella reminds Angelo—mere man, whom his God will in the end call strictly to account, although his subjects may not.[19] He cannot make a single decision at which the Lord is not invisibly present and which He does not weigh and record, as He is said to do in Psalm lxxxii, 1, where, according to Henry Hooke,

> the Prophet David reproving the judges and magistrates of his time . . .
> rippeth up the secret cause of such supine defect in matter of justice:
> They understand nothing, saith he, they know not that God standeth
> as a judge in the middest of their assemblies; therefore, they walk in
> darkness, the eye of their conscience being hoodwinked, that they could
> not see to do equity and judgement.[20]

It is to this text (with all its associations) that Angelo is almost certainly referring when he cries at his exposure:

> I perceive your grace, like pow'r divine,
> Hath look'd upon my passes.
>
> (V. i. 374–5)

As ever in his great Taskmaster's eye, therefore, the ruler must labour to be what God would have him. To begin with, he must be sincerely religious[21]—or, as the Duke puts it in his soliloquy at the end of Act III,

> He who the sword of heaven will bear
> Should be as holy as severe.
>
> (III. ii. 275–6)

[19] Bilson, sigs. C3ᵛ–C4ʳ; James Godskall, *The Kings Medicine for this Present Yeere* (London, 1604), sig. K1ʳ; Smith, *Magistrates Scripture*, pp. 336–7; Jonson, *Panegyre*, sigs. E4ʳ and F1ᵛ; Bullinger, p. 172; Fenton, pp. 57–8, 65–8; James I, *Basilicon Doron*, pp. 17, 95, and *True Lawe*, sigs. B4ʳ, E3ᵛ.

[20] Henry Hooke, *Sermon Preached Before the King* (London, 1604), sig. Bviʳ. See also Bilson, sig. C7ʳ; Perkins, *Treatise*, pp. 86–7; Bullinger, p. 172; Smith, *Memento for Magistrates*, p. 532; Fenton, pp. 66–7; Goslicius, p. 105.

[21] Bilson, sigs. C3ᵛ–C4ʳ; Willet, sig. A4ʳ; Godskall, sigs. N2ᵛ–N3ʳ, G7ᵛ–G8ʳ, K1ʳ; Eedes, sigs. Diᵛ–Diiʳ; Smith, *Magistrates Scripture*, pp. 339–41, 337, and *Memento for Magistrates*, p. 527; Jonson, *Entertainment*, sig. A3ʳ; Sarcerius, fol. ccviᵛ; Gentillet, pp. 97, 357; *Homilies*, sigs. I4ʳ, I5ʳ–I5ᵛ, Pp5ᵛ; Bullinger, pp. 175–6, 184, 187–8; Fenton, pp. 7, 69–71; Goslicius, pp. 100, 104, 107; James I, *Basilicon Doron*, pp. 1–21. See also commentaries on the measure-for-measure passage: Becon, sig. Ddiiiᵛ; Perkins, *Exposition*, p. 424.

Furthermore, he must know and be able to govern himself; for, says Guevara, "when they asked [Thales] what a prince should do to govern others, he answered: he ought first to govern himself, and then afterwards to govern others" [22]—a principle we have already encountered in the commentaries on the mote and the beam and find again in *Measure for Measure*, where it is most clearly stated when the Duke declares in his soliloquy that the ruler must be a man

> More nor less to others paying
> Than by self-offences weighing.
> Shame to him whose cruel striking
> Kills for faults of his own liking!
>   (III. ii. 279–82)

He should also cultivate all the virtues to the best of his ability, but according to the *Basilicon Doron,*

> make one of them, which is Temperance, Queen of all the rest within you. I mean not by the vulgar interpretation of Temperance, which only consists in *gustu & tactu,* by the moderation of these two senses: but I mean of that wise moderation, that first commanding your self, shall as Queen, command all the affections and passions of your mind [p. 84].

Therefore, when Escalus describes the Duke as "one that above all other strifes, contended especially to know himself," and "a gentleman of all temperance" (III. ii. 246–7, 251), what may seem rather faint praise to a modern reader would have been regarded as a very high tribute indeed during the Renaissance. Finally, in all he does, the ruler must remember that his life is the pattern for his subjects, and that, as Richard Eedes explains, "neither are the hearts of the people so easily turned and carried with the dead letter of a written law, as with that life of law, *Justice* living in the life of the prince." [23]

> Pattern in himself to know
> Grace to stand and virtue go,
>   (III. ii. 277–8)

is the way the Duke puts it in his soliloquy.

The more practical and specific duties of the ruler are to get a good

[22] Guevara, 1, 51ᵛ. See also *ibid.* 52ʳ; James I, *Basilicon Doron,* pp. 1–2; Goslicius, p. 106. See also commentaries on the measure-for-measure passage: Erasmus, fol. lxxviiiʳ; Perkins, *Exposition,* p. 424.

[23] Eedes, sigs. Dviiiʳ–Dviiiᵛ. See also Willet, sig. A3ᵛ; Godskall, sig. K1ʳ; Jonson, *Panegyre,* sig. F1ʳ; Gentillet, pp. 99, 279; Smith, *Memento for Magistrates,* p. 532; Fenton, p. 13; Guevara, 1, 50ᵛ; Goslicius, p. 104; James I, *Basilicon Doron,* pp. 3, 23–4, 60–61, and *True Lawe,* sigs. D1ᵛ–D2ʳ.

education, especially in political theory; to love his subjects and be thoroughly acquainted with them—"O how necessary it is," exclaims Guevara, "for a prince to know and understand all things in his Realm, to the end no man might deceive him, as they do nowadays!" (I, 55ʳ); to levy no undue taxes, or waste them when collected—the reciprocal duty of the subject being to pay up cheerfully; to keep peace with all nations if possible, but to protect his own against foreign injury or aggression; to make his laws clear and plain; to choose wise subordinates, control them carefully, and according to Gentillet, let them execute any measures so rigorous that the ruler may be suspected of a purely arbitrary use of his power: "to shun that suspicion and blame, it is good that the prince delegate and set over such matters to Judges, which are good men, not suspected or passionate" (p. 350). It should be noted that this is just what the Duke does in *Measure for Measure*. As he confides to Friar Thomas,

> I have on Angelo impos'd the office,
> Who may in th' ambush of my name strike home,
> And yet my nature never in the fight
> To do it slander.   (I. iii. 40–3)

He also conforms to the Renaissance ideal in loving his subjects and taking steps "to know and understand all things in his Realm, to the end no man might deceive him." His accomplishments in education, taxation, legislation, war, and peace, however, have little bearing on the major issue of the play, and are huddled away under the general statement that "let him be but testimonied in his own bringings-forth, and he shall appear to the envious a scholar, a statesman, and a soldier" (III. ii. 152–5).

But the highest and most important of the ruler's specific duties is to see well to the administration of justice. Here more than anywhere else he and his deputies must act consciously as the substitutes of God; or, in Fenton's words: "the Judges raised by [God] to dispense justice in his place, ought always to have the Majesty of him in their minds, and his judgments in imitation." [24] "They should think," adds Henry Smith, in his *Magistrates Scripture*, "how Christ would judge, before they judge, because God's Law is appointed for their Law" (p. 342). They must not, of course, play favourites, put off decisions, allow their passions to carry them away, accept bribes, give in to fear, be ignorant, listen to slander, or refuse to hear the complaints of the oppressed. But above all, both the chief and the inferior magis-

---

[24] Fenton, p. 64. See also *ibid.* pp. 58–9; Bilson, sig. C7ʳ; Smith, *Magistrates Scripture*, pp. 337, 339–40; Jonson, *Panegyre*, sig. E4ʳ; Bullinger, pp. 152, 194; Guevara, I, 4ʳ–4ᵛ; James I, *Basilicon Doron*, pp. 35, 91, and *True Lawe*, sigs. B3ʳ–B3ᵛ.

trates must cherish the innocent and punish the wicked with all due severity. Bad judges, according to William Perkins' *Treatise on Christian Equity and Moderation,* are of two kinds: the first are

> such men, as by a certain foolish kind of pity are so carried away, that would have nothing but *mercy, mercy,* and would . . . have the extremity of the law executed on no man. This is the high way to abolish laws, and consequently to pull down authority, and so in the end to open a door to all confusion, disorder, and to all licentiousness of life. But I need not say much herein, for there are but few that offend in this kind, man's nature being generally inclined rather to cruelty than to mercy.

The second kind are

> such men as have nothing in their mouths, but the *law,* the *law*: and *Justice, Justice*: in the meantime forgetting that Justice always shakes hands with her sister mercy, and that all laws allow a mitigation. . . . These men, therefore, strike so precisely on their points, and the very tricks and trifles of the law, as (so the law be kept, and that in the very extremity of it) they care not, though equity were trodden under foot: and that law may reign on earth, and they by it: they care not, though mercy take her to her wings, and fly to heaven. These men (for all their goodly shews) are the decayers of our estate, and enemies of all good government.

Mercy and justice, he goes on to say,

> are the two pillars, that uphold the throne of the Prince: as you cannot hold mercy, where Justice is banished, so cannot you keep Justice where mercy is exiled: and as mercy without Justice, is foolish pity, so Justice, without mercy, is cruelty [pp. 15–18].

The same contrast and conclusions drawn by Perkins can be found in many other authorities;[25] and nobody, as far as I know, quarrels with the general principle that mercy should temper justice. The authorities tend, however, to apply it rather narrowly, and only to cases where, as Gentillet cautiously insists, it can "have a good foundation upon reason and equity" (p. 217), as when a man accidentally

---

[25] Eeds, sigs. Eij^r–Eiiij^r, Ei^v–Eii^r; Guevara, III, 3^v; Goslicius, pp. 106–10; James I, *Basilicon Doron,* pp. 29–31; Thomas Blague, *A Sermon . . . Before the Kings Maiestie* (London, 1603), sig. B4^v. The following writers condemn the over-merciful judge, but not the over-severe one: Gentillet, p. 189; *Homilies,* sig. F3^v; Bullinger, pp. 168, 197–8; Fenton, pp. 81–2; and in the commentaries on the measure-for-measure passage: Becon, sigs. Ddiii^v–Ddv^r. The following writers condemn the over-severe judge, but not the over-merciful one: *Two Guides,* sigs. K2^r–K3^v; Bellarmine, pp. 234–5. The general principle that mercy should temper justice is approved by Bilson, sigs. C2^r–C2^v; Gentillet, p. 276; Bullinger, pp. 118, 199; Bellarmine, p. 234; Willet, p. 22; Jonson, *Panegyre,* sig. Fi^r; Hooke, sigs. Diii^v–Div^r; and in the commentaries on the measure-for-measure passage: Becon, sig. Ddiii^v.

kills his friend—the example given by Bullinger (p. 188); or a young
boy steals food because of hunger—the one given by Perkins in his
Treatise (pp. 13–14). No one advocates showing leniency to more
serious or hardened criminals. Since, as we know, Christian forgiveness
was looked on as something apart from public and civil judgment,
it is perhaps hardly surprising to find judicial clemency thus limited
in practice to considerations of ordinary common sense and a reasonable regard for the circumstance of a case. But when we remember
that ideal rulers were also by definition deeply religious men, who
were supposed to "think how Christ would judge, before they judge,"
we cannot help feeling that the theorists have raised a problem to
which they do not give all the attention it deserves. To a lesser de-
gree, this holds true even when they turn to the private individual.
He may, they argue, appeal to the law for the redress of injury, since
God ordained the civil order for that purpose, though as a Christian
he must forgive the malice which accompanied the injury.[26] But as was
probably only natural in an age when personal revenge still enjoyed
a certain amount of social (though not religious) prestige, the great
majority of writers are concerned simply with establishing the tenet
that punishment is the proper business of the civil authorities, to
whom the private individual must leave it. Whether he has any
further practical responsibility for his enemies beyond letting the
law take its course is a question they do not go into. Again, however,
when we remember how eloquently Erasmus Sarcerius, for instance,
can argue (fol. xciv^v) that charity must be extended without reserva-
tion to "friends or enemies, Christians or not Christians . . . according
to the example of the heavenly father, as before is said (Math. v, Luc.
vi)," we are aware of a certain failure to pull the concepts of mercy and
retaliation together—a failure not clearly intentional or obvious, but
present, as it is in the commentaries on the measure-for-measure passage we have already discussed.

Allusions to the measure-for-measure passage occasionally crop up
in the studies of rule, just as references to the doctrine of rule keep
recurring in discussions of the measure-for-measure passage. Guevara,
for example, writes that wicked rulers are like the blind leading the
blind (I, 50^v), and Fenton, that they are like men with motes or beams
in their eyes which prevent them from seeing anything justly (p. 64).
Willymat orders the slanderers of princes to stop judging, "lest (as
Christ Jesus said) you yourselves be judged" (p. 64), while King James
in the *Basilicon Doron* urges his son to give measure for measure, warns
him that he must expect to receive it, and advises him to be faultless because what would be "a mote in another's eye, is a beam in yours"

---

[26] Perkins, *Treatise*, pp. 55–6; Fenton, p. 355; Godskall, sig. K7^r.

(pp. 152, 32, 2). Evidently the passage was one which writers often recalled when working on the doctrine of rule, and frequently brought to the attention of their readers. But Shakespeare would have had special reason to take note of it. The heroine of his plays is a private individual wrestling with the very issues raised by the passage: judgment, tolerance, mercy, retaliation in kind, and Christian forgiveness. His hero and his villain are primarily concerned with the same issues as they appear on a different level—to the holder of public office. His villain has, in addition, just those deficiencies of character which form the clearest and most commonly observed link between the doctrine of rule and the commentaries on the passage. And so, centred as *Measure for Measure* is on the very points at which the two are either parallel or interlocked, it is hardly surprising to find that Shakespeare was apparently influenced to some extent by both.

His treatment of the initial situation seems to have been based in part on the crude but picturesque contrast which the Renaissance theorists so often drew between the two types of bad magistrate. The Duke, at the beginning of the play, would be recognized at once as the type who has failed because he was too merciful to enforce the laws properly. Shakespeare is certainly no Anabaptist—he sees, as clearly as William Perkins himself, the necessity of civil authority, and the terrible picture he paints of Vienna society in decay fully supports Perkins' contention that sentimental pity in a governor merely "opens a door to all confusion, disorder, and to all licentiousness of life." The Duke is essentially a wise and noble man who has erred from an excess of good will; he has put an end to his foolishness before the action proper begins, and so can step gracefully into the role of hero and good ruler; but Shakespeare does not disguise the fact that he has been wrong: he himself frankly describes his laxity as a "vice" (III. ii. 284), and as such any Renaissance audience would certainly consider it.

Angelo, on the other hand, is a perfect case-study in the opposite weakness. Whatever he afterwards becomes, he is not from the first the ordinary venal judge, who is ignorant or cowardly, refuses to hear complaints (for he listens to Isabella), or takes bribes (for his indignation when she unfortunately uses the word sounds quite real); and as she pleads on his behalf at the end of the play:

> A due sincerity governed his deeds,
> Till he did look on me.
>
> (V. i. 451–2)

But he is the epitome of all the men who "have nothing in their mouths but the *law*, the *law*: and *Justice, Justice,* in the meantime forgetting that Justice always shakes hands with her sister mercy." This harshness Shakespeare traces to the personal flaw described in the measure-for-measure passage: the bitter and uncharitable narrowness in judging others that springs from a refusal to recognize or deal with one's own faults. Unlike the Duke, Angelo has not contended especially to know himself; he has no real conception of the potentialities of his own character. As a result, he thinks so well of himself that he neither has any defence against sudden overwhelming temptation nor possesses the humility and comprehension necessary to deal properly with Claudio.

His treatment of Claudio is from the first inexcusable, even by the strict standards of the Renaissance. For clemency in this particular case would certainly have had "a good foundation upon reason and equity": Claudio and Juliet are betrothed; they fully intend to marry; they are penitent; and the law was drowsy and neglected when they broke it. Furthermore, Claudio comes of a good family; and his fault is, after all, a very natural one. Shakespeare wisely leaves these last points to be made by Escalus and the Provost, both kind, sensible men who represent the normal point of view and whose support of Claudio is therefore significant. But Isabella cannot treat the offence lightly without weakening both the dignity of her calling and the force of her horror at Angelo's proposal. So in the first scene where she implores him for her brother's life, she bases her plea chiefly on modulations and variations of the two great Christian arguments we have already encountered in discussions of the measure-for-measure passage, interwoven with appropriate material from the doctrine of rule. The first is most clearly stated when, after pointing out that clemency is considered a virtue in the ruler, she begs him to remember that we must be merciful, as the Father was also merciful in redeeming us:

> Why, all the souls that were were forfeit once,
> And he that might the vantage best have took
> Found out the remedy. How would you be
> If he which is the top of judgement should
> But judge you as you are? O, think on that!
> And mercy then will breathe within your lips
> Like man new-made.   (II. ii. 73–9)

And then, after reminding him that a ruler is only a man dressed in a little brief authority, she urges him to think of his own faults before he condemns Claudio's:

> Go to your bosom,
> Knock there and ask your heart what it doth know
> That's like my brother's fault. If it confess

>   A natural guiltiness such as is his,
>   Let it not sound a thought upon your tongue
>   Against my brother's life.   (II. ii. 136–41)

But it should be noted that she does not threaten him with retaliation
in kind for his cruelty. Indeed, in her eagerness to show him that
it *is* cruelty and to convince him that he ought to do as he would be
done by, she argues rather that she in his place would not be so
severe:

>   I would to heaven I had your potency
>   And you were Isabel! Should it then be thus?
>   No! I would tell what 'twere to be a judge,
>   And what a prisoner.   (II. ii. 66–9)

Her problem is not, however, to be quite such a simple one. Angelo's
next move is not to throw himself on her kindness, but attempt to
take advantage of it. If she is truly so merciful, he implies, she should
be willing to rescue Claudio even at the expense of breaking what the
Renaissance regarded as a most sacred law of God, and one doubly
binding upon her because she is not only a virgin but a novice: if
she refuses,

>   Were you not then as cruel as the sentence
>   That you have slandered so?   (II. iv. 109–10)

The modern reader may find it difficult not to echo this question,
particularly when Claudio himself breaks down and adds the weight
of his own desperate pleading to Angelo's arguments. Why, after all
her talk of charity and forbearance, should Isabella not only decline
to save her brother's life by an act of generosity, but condemn him
so unsparingly for begging her to do so? When, however, we remember
the limitations which Renaissance doctrine set on both charity and
forbearance, we have no right to assume that Shakespeare is deliberately and cynically implying that his heroine is, in her own way,
as narrow and cold as his villain. He seems rather to be trying to
emphasize and illustrate the familiar tenet that neither charity nor
forbearance must be carried to the point of permitting or condoning
outrage. Like the Duke on the public level, Isabella is not entitled to
let Angelo and Claudio use her mercy as their bawd; and, as the commentators on the measure-for-measure passage had made clear, her
"duty is not to wink at them, but to take notice of them, and to show
open dislike of them." Claudio is such a pathetic figure, and his horror
of death so dreadfully comprehensible, that it may be fair to wonder
if Shakespeare, when writing the prison scene, was not momentarily
caught in what Tucker Brooke would call one of his conflicts of

"intuitive sympathy with predetermined form";[27] but there is no evidence that he or his audience would not have felt Isabella's conduct was both demanded and justified by the ethical pattern of the play as he had consciously established it.

The conspiracy which follows also has its place in that pattern. It takes the form of a deliberate infliction upon Angelo of like for like, as the Duke is at pains to inform the audience in his soliloquy:

> So disguise shall, by th' disguised
> Pay with falsehood false exacting
> (III. ii. 294–5)

—offence punishing offence just as it is said to do in the measure-for-measure passage and the commentaries upon it. It should be noted, however, that the responsibility for devising and managing the whole plot rests on the shoulders of the Duke, who has a ruler's right to see to retaliation in kind and a ruler's privilege of using extraordinary means to ensure the success of a worthy cause. The part which Isabella necessarily plays in the conspiracy is as far as possible minimized: we are not allowed actually to see her persuading Mariana, reporting to Angelo, or doing anything but simply agreeing to the scheme because it is presented to her as the only sure way to save Claudio, protect herself, right Mariana, and secure any real evidence against the deputy. Unlike the Duke, she acts from no special desire to pay Angelo back in his own coin; it is only afterwards, when she hears the news of Claudio's death by his treachery, that she breaks down and very understandably cries for personal and immediate revenge: "O, I will to him and pluck out his eyes!" (IV. iii. 124). The calmer Duke then very properly persuades her that she ought instead to turn her cause over to the civil authorities:

> And you shall have your bosom on this wretch,
> Grace of the Duke, revenges to your heart,
> And general honour.   (IV. iii. 139–41)

The audience at the first performance of the play probably took this promise at its face-value, as a prediction that Angelo was to suffer full legal punishment for his offences in the trial to come. Nor would they have disapproved. His case is very different from Claudio's. His judge, the Duke, is not, as he was, unfit for his task; and he cannot plead for mercy "with a good foundation upon reason and equity," as Claudio could. Although he has not actually succeeded in doing the worst he intended to do, there is still a heavy count against him:

[27] Tucker Brooke, "The Renaissance," in *A Literary History of England,* ed. A. C. Baugh (New York, 1948), p. 527.

attempted seduction, abuse of his authority, deception of his prince, and treachery of the meanest kind; while if he *had* done what he himself and every character on the stage except the Duke believes that he has, there was nothing to be said against the Duke's sentence:

> The very mercy of the law cries out
> Most audible, even from his proper tongue,
> "An Angelo for Claudio, death for death."
> Haste still pays haste, and leisure answers leisure;
> Like doth quit like, and Measure still for Measure. . . .
> We do condemn thee to the very block
> Where Claudio stooped to death, and with like haste.
>
> (V. i. 412–20)

The audience, knowing what they knew, probably did not expect that the execution would really take place; but they can hardly have been prepared for what actually follows. First, Mariana, still pathetically devoted to her husband, begs the Duke for his life; and then, failing, she turns to Isabella—who is not in love with Angelo, who has every good reason to loathe him, who might plead with justice that his punishment is now entirely a matter for the civil authorities —and begs for her help.

The cruelty of the appeal is obvious; and the natural, the instinctive, and (we must remember) the allowed reply to it is implicit in the shocked exclamation of the Duke:

> Against all sense you do importune her.
> Should she kneel down, in mercy of this fact,
> Her brother's ghost his paved bed would break,
> And take her hence in horror.   (V. i. 438–41)

Then Mariana cries out to Isabella again—and she kneels, not in silence, which is all Mariana dares to ask for, but generously to make the best case she can for Angelo. Her act is not natural; it is not (as the Duke has carefully pointed out) even reasonable: it is sheer, reckless forgiveness of the kind Christ advocates in the Sermon on the Mount—the great pronouncement which in Luke immediately precedes and forms part of the measure-for-measure passage. And like Christ, Shakespeare contrasts this sort of forgiveness with another. Mariana is certainly more praiseworthy than the "sinners" described by the Lord, for Angelo has treated her very badly; but her mercy to him resembles theirs in that it springs primarily from preference and affection: she loves her lover (to quote the common sixteenth-century translation of Luke vi, 32) and she hopes for something again—the renewal of his devotion and a happy marriage with him. Hence, how-

ever gracious and commendable her conduct may be, it differs mark-
edly from that of Isabella, who has nothing to sustain her but the
conviction that she *must* be merciful and the memory of what she
had promised Angelo on the strength of it. And then, almost before
the audience at the first performance had time to catch its breath,
the Duke, having summoned Claudio and revealed the truth, proceeds
not only to pardon him, but to let off Angelo, Lucio, and Barnardine
as well, with penalties entirely disproportionate to what their conduct
deserved by ordinary Renaissance standards.

We may, if we please, argue that Shakespeare suddenly remembered
he was writing a comedy and decided he had better botch up some
sort of happy ending to send the audience home contented, regardless
of probability and doctrine alike. But all the evidence goes to show
that the audience would have left for home equally contented—perhaps even more contented—if Angelo, Lucio, and Barnardine had
been punished, like Shylock, or remanded for judgment at some future
date, like Don John in *Much Ado about Nothing*. And when we recall
the special difficulties and defects of Renaissance doctrine, it seems at
least possible that the conclusion of *Measure for Measure* may rather
represent a deliberate effort—perhaps a little clumsy, certainly romantic—to "do something" about that disturbing discrepancy between
the concepts of religious mercy and secular justice which we find in
the commentaries on the measure-for-measure passage and again in the
studies of rule. Like the theorists, Shakespeare was apparently prepared
to concede that the private Christian should not (in the name of
mercy) weakly condone every form of injustice and oppression, and
may, if necessary, invoke secular authority to defend what he knows
to be right. But it is not enough merely to wash his hands of personal
revenge, and—let the secular authority do the dirty work for him.
Nor should the secular authority himself forget that "judging as
Christ would judge" means something more than weighing each case
according to common sense and ordinary good will. He need not make
a scarecrow of the law: he must be vigilant to suppress or prevent disorder and evil; and he should see to it that the innocent are properly
protected—that Isabella's name is cleared by her traducer; that Barnardine is committed to the friar instead of being turned loose on
society; that Claudio makes amends to Juliet, Angelo to Mariana,
Lucio to the girl he has wronged. He may even, to a certain extent,
use retaliation in kind, or the threat of retaliation in kind, to bring
malefactors to their senses: it is no accident that Angelo is paid with
falsehood false exacting, or finds himself sentenced to the very block
where Claudio stooped to death, and with like haste. But his primary
duty is, like God, to show mercy whenever he possibly can, even when
the fault is disgusting and the criminal despicable: to remember that

Lucio's slanders hurt chiefly the Duke's own personal feelings; that
Barnardine is a mere animal,

> A creature unprepared, unmeet for death;
> And to transport him in the mind he is
> Were damnable;   (IV. iii. 71-3)

that Angelo has been blasted and shamed out of his appalling com-
placency, and may, as Mariana pleads: "become much more the better/
For being a little bad" (V. i. 445-6). It is the difference between the
"Like doth quit like" with which the Duke begins his sentence on
his deputy and the "Well, Angelo, your evil quits you well," with
which he concludes it.

In all this, Shakespeare is not so much rejecting the ordinary Christian doctrine of the Renaissance as clarifying it, strengthening it, and
holding it true to its own deepest implications. Just how or when he
formed his own opinions on the question there is no telling. We do
not know what books he read or what sermons he attended, although
we should note that he could have picked up practically all the
necessary doctrinal instruction from reading two books or hearing
two sermons that interested him, while the agreement between the
various authorities makes it certain that the theories he was taught
would not differ drastically from the ones we have already summed up
and discussed. The investigation, however, sheds no light on his own
denominational preferences; he touches in this play only on such
elements of traditional theology as were shared by Anglican, Puritan,
and Roman Catholic alike. Nor, since to dramatize a doctrine is not
necessarily to believe in it, are we entitled to use *Measure for Measure*
as evidence that he himself was even a Christian. All that can be said
with safety is that when he put his mind to it, he could produce a
more coherent, a more independent, and in the last analysis, a more
Christian piece of thinking on the subject than nine out of ten professional Renaissance theologians.

Philosophy and Theatre in
Measure for Measure

by Francis Fergusson

I suppose that in our efforts to understand Shakespeare, what we seek is a grasp of his plays as plays. We want his theater to come fully alive before us; we wish to hear and to understand as fully as possible the complex harmonies which we now believe are there.

Forty or fifty years ago a kind of "higher criticism" of Shakespeare was in vogue, which had the effect of disintegrating the plays and obscuring or denying their coherence. The corruption of the texts was emphasized, and Shakespeare's authorship was questioned in whole or in part. His dramaturgy was compared, to his disadvantage, with Ibsen's. His psychology, when it did not seem to agree with modern notions, was dismissed as faulty or irresponsible. When Shaw proclaimed that Shakespeare lacked *his* up-to-date enlightenment he merely confirmed a widespread prejudice. The spirit in which we now read Shakespeare seems to me much healthier. We are less in love with our own clichés; less sure of our psychological insight; less fascinated with the well-made plot, and more interested in the culture of the Renaissance and the Middle Ages, which, at the very least, provided Shakespeare with indispensable *means* to his great work. And so we are able, once more, to accept him as a still-living master of the theater and of the lore of the human psyche; and we assume that the ultimate purpose of our scholarship and criticism is rather to learn from him than merely to learn *about* him.

Measure for Measure is one of the plays which has suffered most from the habit of judging Shakespeare on extrinsic grounds, and it is one of the plays which has benefited most from our new awareness of his perennial wisdom and artistry. For this reason it is not in the

least original to say (as I propose to do) that *Measure for Measure* has
a great deal to offer us. Nevertheless it is still puzzling, for it is not
exactly like anything else which Shakespeare wrote. Is it a kind of
morality play, like *Everyman*? Is it a problem play, or a thesis-play, as
Mr. W. W. Lawrence suggested? Or what kind of composition is it?

My general thesis is that it is to be understood as both philosophy
and poetry-of-the-theater, but that the two are not separate, or merely
mechanically combined, but two cognate modes of presenting a single
underlying vision of man in society. But, if so, then the philosophy
must be something quite unlike our contemporary academic philosophy.
And the poetry-of-the-theater is not what we usually mean by poetry,
for our conception of this art is derived from the modern lyric, the
lyric since Baudelaire perhaps; and we know that our best lyricists
distrust all the uses of the mind but the lyric inspiration itself.
Shakespeare's philosophy and theatricality emerged from another
tradition—one which tends to be lost to sight—and in approaching
Measure for Measure we must remember a little of what that tradition
contained.

I begin with a few remarks on the nature of the "philosophy" in
this play.

The Duke, in his first speech, which begins the play, says to Escalus,

> Of government the properties to unfold
> Would seem, in me, to affect speech and discourse.

The Duke in fact will not unfold the properties of government in
speech and discourse alone. But the play which follows, when the Duke
has disappeared and Angelo is ruler, will unfold them, both dramatically and in the dialectic of Angelo, Isabella, and Lucio. The Duke, as
Friar, will observe and explain this unfolding, and in the last act,
having resumed his authority as Duke, he will demonstrate the same
philosophy of government and its properties in the trials and judgments of all the characters.

The title of the play suggests the mystery of human government
which the drama explores in one way and the philosophy in another:
that of the relation between Justice and Mercy, or Charity. "Measure
for Measure" may mean either weight for weight, an eye for an eye
and a tooth for a tooth, or it may mean a measure of measurement
itself: that is, Charity, which measures or proportions the strict justice
of human reason seeking mathematical rigor.

The late Theodore Spencer, and more recently Mr. Tillyard, has
shown that in Shakespeare's time the medieval tradition, with its com-
bination of Greek thought and Christian religion, was still very much
alive. Mr. I. A. Richards has pointed out many echoes of Platonic

philosophy in Shakespeare's plays, notably in *Troilus and Cressida.* These and other writers have made it clear that, whatever Shakespeare may have read or believed, this complx philosophic heritage was somehow available to him and to the cultivated part of his audience. If one looks at the *Basilikon Doron* of James I—whom some believe to have been the model for the Duke—one can see that the monarch was thinking about justice and mercy, spiritual and temporal authority, and indeed all the properties of government, with the same philosophic background as we find in *Measure for Measure.*

In attempting to understand the philosophy in this play, therefore, one must remember the classic formulations, both Greek and Christian, which were then current. Mr. G. Wilson Knight, in his fine essay, interprets the play as a straight allegory of New Testament morality. There is no doubt that this element is there, and extremely important. St. Paul's distinction between Mosaic Law, with its rational and literal justice, and the new rule of Charity (or Mercy, as the Hebrew prophets put it) pervades the play. But so, I think, does the Platonic and Aristotelian philosophy of society, which is based upon the analogy between the body politic and the individual, whose life has many modes, vegetable, animal, rational, and whose body has many organs serving the whole in different ways. Because this philosophy recognizes the diversity of man in a social whole, it produces an *analogical* conception of justice, which is almost as far from Mosaic literal and univocal justice as Charity itself is. This Greek tradition was essential in building that central, catholic philosophy of government which Shakespeare's contemporaries—James himself, [and] Hooker—were endeavoring to oppose to the rationalized revolutionary and counter-revolutionary movements of the time: to Puritanism, to Jesuitism, and in a later generation to the single-minded absolutism of a Hobbes. Thus "the nature of our people and our city's institutions," as the Duke puts it, are the very matter of the play's philosophy. In the mirror of the Duke's "Vienna," and in the light of the Greek-Christian tradition, the play reveals the actual drama of government in Shakespeare's own city.

If these observations are acceptable, it follows that the philosophy in this play is not a theory, or a neat system of logically connected concepts, but *philosophia,* the love of wisdom. This love of wisdom, embodied in the order of society and in the literary heritage, had been fed by a tradition going back through the Middle Ages and St. Augustine to the Greeks and to the Bible. And so Shakespeare can use the ancient formulations as commonplaces, *topoi,* means or occasions for communicating his own view of the perennial mystery.

Mr. W. W. Lawrence called *Measure for Measure* a "problem comedy." He was thinking of the contemporary play of ideas or theses, of Ibsen, Shaw, even Brieux. He was, however, not very happy with this comparison, and no wonder, for it is of the essence of our problem plays that the central wisdom is lacking, and, therefore, that the theses of the reformers are all the thought they have to offer. Shakespeare has no thesis, no "platform," in that sense—he leaves that kind of thinking to his Angelos and his Isabellas. He is not, in fact, solving a problem so much as he is setting forth, from many points of view, an ineluctable mystery in human affairs.

It is only philosophy in the ancient sense of *philosophia* which can come from the same sources of insight as narrative, character, poetry-of-the-theater. And it is only a sophisticated version of poetry-of-the-theater which can recognize the source it may have in common with the love of wisdom. I proceed to a few observations on this knowing theatricality as Shakespeare used it.

Everyone knows that Shakespeare made his plays out of histories, stories, and even other plays. *Measure for Measure* is made from the story and the play of Promos and Cassandra, to which Shakespeare added the traditional bed-trick, which has offended so many, and the ancient theme of the ruler who (like Harun-al-Rashid) visits and observes his people in disguise. All of these tales were old and familiar, and, as many writers have pointed out, such old familiar tales had been accepted since the Middle Ages as having some sort of meaning or truth, some light to throw upon human nature and destiny. They constituted a sort of secular mythology for Renaissance Europe; and for Shakespeare they provided, like the philosophic themes in *Measure for Measure*, themes or topics or commonplaces of another kind. It was his practice to combine, vary, and develop them to make the rich texture of his stage play.

The philosophic themes of *Measure for Measure* are to be found in the structure of the play, in the discourses of the Duke, and in the dialectic of Angelo, Isabella and Lucio. The debates reveal Shakespeare's familiarity with Renaissance-Aristotelian logic and rhetoric, as Sister Miriam Joseph has shown. The narrative themes, on the other hand, are developed dramatically by the players. Shakespeare uses the situations and the main events of the old stories very much as exercises in good acting schools, in which the actors are taught to improvise plays on situations given by the instructor. Thus, given the departure of the Duke and the new authority of Angelo, what will happen? The players will show us, making-believe the given characters and situations, and following out with full concentration and consistency the terrible or pathetic results. In short, the traditional tales which Shakespeare used were publicly acceptable means whereby his players could "hold the mirror up to nature."

If one thinks of Shakespeare's stories in this way, one can, I think, understand their apparent artificiality. Would Lear, really, have given his kingdom away to his daughters? Would the Duke really have embarked on that romantic project of departure and return in disguise? I do not know; but I see that in each case the initial situation is the basic *donné,* or call it the working hypothesis, of the whole play. The significance is to be found (as in an experiment in the laboratory) in the working out of the vital results of this made-believe situation. And I am sure that the very *arbitrariness* of this basic *donné* is essential: it establishes that concrete, fated, unrationalizable element in human affairs without which there can be no actual life and no drama. Because Shakespeare had these accepted tales, with all their inexplicable concreteness, he had a means of reflecting the intimate actuality of human life before or beneath all theory.

Thus I think that the philosophizing and the playing in *Measure for Measure* spring from the same source, show the same "habits of mind and feeling," and embody the same cultivated awareness of man in society. I should say that the style of the play as a whole was at once rational and poetic. But this is a style with which we are not very familiar, in contemporary drama or literature, and to understand it one must think of a very few masters, high points in the tradition, who had attained a comparable balance and flexibility.

I have already mentioned Plato. The dialectic in the great dialogues does not move toward the univocal concept; it is not resolved by deciding between two contradictory propositions, but by the appearance of a new insight, which transcends and in a way includes both sides. In this process the characters, and their interplay, are as important as the play of concepts; and when an anecdote or a parable is introduced, we do not feel that the subject is being changed, but rather that it is being presented in a complementary way. The whole is sustained and lightened by a spirit of play or significant make-believe, which we feel both in the actions of the characters and in the hypotheses to be discussed. I feel a similar sophisticated and resourceful style in the central cantos of the *Purgatorio,* where Vergil and Marco Lombardo expound the traditional philosophy of man in society, the issues of justice and mercy, of temporal and spiritual authority, against the darkness of anger and the darkness of Italian policies, which Dante and Marco so sharply recall. In such works, as in *Measure for Measure,* we are invited to play the poetry and the philosophy off against each other, illuminating the actual tangle of human affairs with wisdom, yet never losing the distinction between the general truths of philosophy and the concrete realities of life.

But this is more than enough by way of general observations. I

now wish to suggest a reading of the play. For this purpose I shall
follow one thread only in the complex pattern, that of the role of the
Duke.

The Duke has displeased many critics, who report either that he is
not a character at all, but merely a *deus ex machina,* or else that he
is a liar, weakling and hypocrite. The Duke is puzzling, and perhaps
ultimately not quite successful. But it is certain that he is the center
of the play, and the clue to its intention and its peculiar style. Shakespeare did not find him in the Promos-Cassandra play, but added him,
to give that old story a new form and meaning. He made the Duke
both a character within the play who takes a crucial part in the
struggle, and at the same time a sort of stage director, who because of
his power and wisdom can start and control the action as though
from the wings. It is a question whether we can accept this double
function, and believe in the Duke both within and above the story.
But at least we may investigate the theatrical and philosophic purpose
of such a creation.

Let us consider first his character within the story, that of the eccentric
Duke of Vienna. W. W. Lawrence (who on the whole takes the play
pretty literally) points out that he represents the authority of both
Church and State, as he plays Friar and Duke. He thinks that he is a
conventional figure, especially at the end of the play, when, like many
a prince or priest, he winds up the plot and points the moral. This
conventional element is there, no doubt, but we must remember how
lively the issues of spiritual and temporal authority were in the early
years of James I's reign; even in the playhouse they must have meant
more than a romantic convention. James himself took his responsibility
as guide and leader of his people with pedantic seriousness. He would
have agreed with Marco Lombardo that both spiritual and temporal
rulers have the duty of showing the people *della vera cittade almen la
torre,* "at least the tower of the true city." The Duke is such a ruler:
he wishes to *teach* Vienna the properties of government. That is the
clue to his action in the play, and also to his *régisseur's* action outside
the play: he wishes to show London the properties of government in
the experimental situation of Vienna.

If the Duke is understood as a teacher, his supposed deviousness
and hypocrisy is explained, for he is a very modest and empirical
kind of teacher. He would understand the force of Plato's or St.
Augustine's dicta, that a teacher can only help the student to realize
what he knew already. He anticipates our progressive educators, who
maintain that one can really learn only "by doing." Mr. Donald Stauffer
(in *Shakespeare's World of Images*) describes the Duke's pedagogical
style as follows:

The Duke of dark corners sets a number of problems as experiments which various characters must work out for their own salvation. The Duke prefers the laboratory to the lecture-room. Shakespeare returns to his conviction that experience is the best teacher, that painful experience may be deliberately intensified in order to assure a clearer acknowledgment of error; that realization, remorse, repentance, and a change of heart are unavoidable steps in moral betterment.

When the Duke departs and leaves Angelo in charge, he sets the city a practical problem in government. The city unfolds the properties of government by trying all the wrong moves; and the Duke is at hand to reinforce the painful lessons in his counsel to Isabella or to Claudio, and at last by the order which, as temporal ruler, he can impose. In all of this, his role is a figure and an analogue of that of Shakespeare, who set up the situation of the old Promos-Cassandra story, guided its development, and interpreted it in the light of his own traditional philosophy of government.

Most students of *Measure for Measure* find the first three acts the best. It is there that we most unmistakably recognize poetry, drama, the natural movement and variety of life as in Shakespeare's greatest tragedies. And it is there that the Duke takes the least active part. Having set the stage for a tragedy by handing his city over to the tyrannical perfectionist Angelo, he merely observes, and explains in secrecy to the characters whose suffering might bear fruit in wisdom.

Shakespeare and the Duke clearly intended this effect, as the first part of their demonstration. They wished to show to Vienna, and to London in the mirror of Vienna, a tragedy in the making: a city hopelessly divided between the doctrinaire perfectionism of Angelo and Isabella, the innocent sensuality of Claudio, and the cynical sophistication of Lucio, the whole placed against a background of the weaknesses, fears and darkness of routine human nature as we see it in any corrupt old city. The nascent tragedy which results is wonderfully suggestive for us also. I see in it a theme like Yeats's "The centre cannot hold,/Mere anarchy is loosed upon the world." The Duke, with his wisdom and power, represents the missing center. Angelo and Isabella, with their ambitious intellectuality, represent revolutionary or counter-revolutionary forces, which change their policies but not their narrow power drives, as they struggle in the dark and empty center. Of course the debates are in the theological terms of Shakespeare's time, but our contemporary tragedies of the dissolving center are strikingly similar in their *dramatic* form.

In this nascent tragedy Lucio is the counterpart of the Duke, and thus throws a great deal of light upon him. Lucio has a talent for chaos as great as the Duke for wisdom or the central order. Shakespeare uses Lucio in the first two acts as the chief reflector of the action, to use Henry James's valuable term: it is through Lucio's intelligent and faithless eyes that we grasp what is going on. In Act I, scene 2, he explains the first impact of Angelo's inhuman strictness upon the easy-going and corrupt humanity of Vienna, with bawdy wit spiced with theological learning. He bids us appreciate the poetry in which Claudio, on the way to execution, expresses his plight:

> Our natures do pursue,
> Like rats that ravin down their proper bane,
> A thirsty evil, and when we drink we die.

"If I could speak so wisely under an arrest I would send for certain of my creditors," says Lucio, with urbanity. And it is he who both appreciates and dismisses Isabella, the green novice, when he hails her as "a thing ensky'd and sainted." The image is, I think, that of the plaster saint. Isabella feels it a mockery, and the mockery is deepened through the implicit contrast with Julietta, whom Lucio next describes in the beautiful lines,

> As those that feed grow full, as blossoming time
> That from the seedness the bare fallow brings
> To teeming foison, even so her plenteous womb
> Expresseth his full tilth and husbandry.

Above all, it is Lucio who arranges the fight between Angelo and Isabella, and interprets it for us, blow by blow, with the most refined psychological insight. It was his inspiration to "bait the hook with a saint in order to catch a saint," as Angelo says, with terror, when he sees how he is caught. He suggests that Lucio is more than the devil's advocate, almost the devil himself.

At the end of the play Lucio is the only character whom the Duke cannot really forgive. Shall we say that Lucio has insight without integrity? Or that he represents treachery, which Shakespeare, like Dante, hates above all other sins? Or that he is only a trimmer like Rosencrantz and Guildenstern, a "private of fortune," neither for good nor for evil but only for his trivial self? However that may be, Lucio has things his own way in the first half of the play, encouraging the unregenerate appetites of all the characters, using his imagination in the service of darkness, while the Duke keeps his true power hidden. But in the middle of Act III the Duke begins to take an active part, and thenceforth Lucio is out of his depth and can no longer interpret the action for us. The tragedy is arrested on the very brink of catastrophe, and the end of the play presents the mystery of justice and mercy in a way undreamed of in Lucio's philosophy.

Readers of *Measure for Measure* who like the first three acts usually dislike the last two, when the Duke asserts his authority to restore order. They miss the completion of the tragic sequence as we find it in *Macbeth* or *Hamlet* or *Othello*. In the fourth act, in those great works, evil both triumphs and ends: Othello caves in under Iago's lies, Macbeth and his lady taste the fruit of futility and fear, Claudius's regime breaks up in scandal and confusion. In the fifth act the vision of evil is complete against a good which is implicit or announced as coming. In *Measure for Measure* the Duke arrests the course of evil and presents the good, or the order of wisdom, more directly and at length. So we are balked of our tragedy; but do we get an adequate ending to the play in a different key?

The Duke starts to intervene when he proposes the bed-trick to Isabella. In Act IV his plans proceed with great speed. The timing is close, and the language is prose, as though Shakespeare by this change of rhythm, this sudden deflation and sobriety in speech, were warning us that playtime is over, the citizens have been given their head long enough, and now we must pay attention to matters of a different kind of seriousness. I find this change of key successful: there is poetic power in the sequence in the prison, at night, with the Duke working against time to avert catastrophe and accept his sober responsibility for his flock. But the act is very brief, a modulation from the nascent tragedy of the first three acts to the complex demonstration of Act V. Just before abandoning his role as Friar, the Duke warns us what to expect in the final part of his play: "By cold gradation and well-balanced form," he says, "we shall proceed with Angelo."

It has often been maintained that Act V is a mere perfunctory windup of the plot, in which Shakespeare himself had no real interest. I am sure that on the contrary it is composed with the utmost care, and in perfect consistency with the basis of the whole play—this quite apart from the question whether one *likes* it or not. It is indeed so beautifully composed that it could almost stand alone. Perhaps we should think of it as a play within a play, presenting the theme of justice and mercy in another story and in another and colder tone. But the new story—that of the Duke's intervention and demonstration —was implicit from the first; and the new cold, intellectual tone may be understood as underneath the more richly poetic manner of the first three acts.

We are invited to watch this last act with a kind of double vision: from the front of the house, and at the same time from the wings, where we can see the actors getting ready to pretend to be what they are not. For, like the Duke, we know what they are; and moreover we have seen the Duke's backstage preparations for the final play. This final public play, unrolling before us and the supposedly ignorant Duke, is in the form of a series of trials. The first begins with Isabella's desperate complaint of Angelo, and ends when her suit is rejected on the basis of the evidence then publicly available: the wild improbability of her story, and Angelo's fine reputation and dignified manner. The second trial starts when the Duke leaves Angelo and Escalus to try Isabella for her supposed lying slander, and it ends when the Duke returns in his Friar disguise as a witness, and is suddenly revealed as the Duke when Lucio pulls off his hood. The third part ends both trials: the Duke, now revealed as both judge and witness, metes out justice to all, but on the assumption which we know to be false, that Claudio is dead. Notice that up to this point the trials and judgments have obeyed the strictest reasoned conception of justice, and the facts insofar as they could be found under the frightened and passionate lies in which they had been hidden. The Duke has been following a Mosaic regularity, and he has also been acting like that image of justice as a woman with bandaged eyes, a pair of scales in one hand and a sword in the other. He had been pretending to rely, not upon his concrete vision, but upon reportable "facts" and his abstract measuring-machine. But in the final act of this playlet the Duke as it were drops the bandage from his eyes, confesses what he can really see, starting with the fact that Claudio is alive. He then tempers or proportions justice with mercy, abstract reason with his perception of the analogical relationships between real people, in whom truth and error, sin and grace, are mingled in ways which mathematics cannot compute.

I offer this sketch of Act V, not as exhausting its complexities, but to support my view that it is composed with the greatest care and the most self-conscious art. But some of its critics say that it is not poetry, not the proper end of a poetic drama, but only philosophy or abstract allegory. And indeed it is certain that when the Duke establishes an order in accordance with his own wisdom, we have a new relation between the dramatic and philosophic developments of the theme of justice and mercy.

Thus it is possible to read this act as an allegory of the descent of Mercy upon the scene of human judgment. The Duke, like God, comes not to destroy the Law—for he uses it to demonstrate everyone's guilt—but to transcend it. His role throughout the play is like that of Grace, in its various forms, as theologians describe it: he works through the repentant Mariana and Claudio to illuminate their motives and prevent their follies; and here at the end he answers Mariana's prayer after the intercession of Isabella. These relationships are worked out with theological scrupulousness, and I suppose that Shakespeare must have been aware of the possibility of this interpretation.

But at the same time he presents the Duke, not as God or as a mere symbol of a theological concept, but as a real human being; and Act V may be read, therefore, as the end of a *drama*. Mariana's love for Angelo had sharpened her insight: she was able to see through his actual savagery to the bewildered spirit within, which still had the potentialities of good; and the Duke, as Friar, had encouraged her in this strength, charity and understanding. Isabella had a wise *doctrine* from the first, but this doctrine remained helpless and disembodied until she was matured by suffering and appealed to by Mariana. In short, the play has shown how the wisdom of love proceeded from the Duke to the two women, to be finally confirmed by him when they reveal it at the end. Such is the *drama* of the growth of wisdom in Vienna, which finally reverses the tragic course toward anarchy. Angelo sees it coming, as knowledge of the truth, before Mercy supervenes; he is caught and stopped in his tracks as by a sudden glare of light:

> I should be guiltier than my guiltiness
> To think I can be undiscernible
> When I perceive your Grace, like power divine,
> Has look'd upon my passes.

Dante's Vergil has a phrase which accurately describes such a growth of understanding in human terms: "Love kindled by virtue," he says, "always kindles another, if only its flame shows outwardly." Vergil is of course a pagan, and he is thinking of the relationships between himself, Statius, and Dante, whose love was shown outwardly in their writings. The point is that Shakespeare's eye, as usual, was upon the reality of human experience, where the life of drama is.

Moreover, he has written Act V with its own theatrical poetry, which one may miss if one does not think of its actual stage effects. It is not only a series of trials and a demonstration of the Duke's wise authority; it is also a masquerade, a play of pretense and illusion. As we watch it with what I have called our "double vision," we can see each character in turn compelled to relinquish his pretense, his public costume. And in this respect Act V merely carries to its conclusion one of the important theater-poetic themes of the whole play, that of human life itself as a dream or masquerade. Angelo expresses it when he says,

> . . . my gravity,
> Wherein, let no man hear me, I take pride,
> Could I with boot change for an idle plume
> Which the air beats for vain. O Place! O Form!

How often dost thou, with thy case, thy habit,
Wrench awe from fools, and tie the wiser souls
To thy false seeming!

Isabella echoes this when she calls Angelo "seeming, seeming!" and in her vision of man, "most ignorant of what he's most assured,/His glassy essence." The Duke's great speech to Claudio in prison, "Be absolute for death," plays many variations on this theme, for instance:

Thou art not thyself;
For thou exist'st on many a thousand grains
That issue out of dust. . . .

. . . thy complexion shifts to strange effects
After the moon. . . .

Thou hast nor youth nor age,
But as it were an after-dinner's sleep,
Dreaming on both.

In the first three acts we are in the midst of these masquerades; we are moved by their seductive passion and music. In the last act, playtime over, the music changes, the masques are put aside, and we are shown what Shakespeare evidently regarded as the underlying truth of the human situation.

It is our contemporary habit to believe that "the masquerades which time resumes" (as Eliot puts it) *are* the reality of the human situation. And so the shimmering detail of Shakespeare's theater-poetry is likely to be enough for us; we do not often enquire how it is *composed,* what underlying action governs the form and the movement of the play as a whole. But, because Shakespeare did compose his plays, he must in some sense have seen deeper than the passions, the delusions, the imaginative exuberance which make the incomparable *immediate* life of his theater. He would probably have agreed with Pico della Mirandola about the power and also the danger of Imagination, when not controlled by a deeper vision of the intellect. That is why, in *Measure for Measure,* he can move so freely between theater-poetry and dialectic as two modes of presenting action, the psyche's life. And that, I believe, is why he can present the Duke's demonstration in Act V as the end both of the thought and of the poetic play.

This brings me to my final point, the question of the success of the role of the Duke. Can we accept him, or is he simply too wise and good and powerful to work in a play?

I must admit that I know no simple answer to this question. It would depend upon the innumerable circumstances of a performance;

the skill and understanding of the actors, the taste and prejudices of the audience. But I think I see why Shakespeare could have wished to make such a character, who would be both inside the play, and so subject to its fictive situation, and also visible *outside* it, controlling and interpreting its course. He wished to show the *making* of the play at the same time as the play itself. So he presents Vienna, not as literal reporting in the manner of modern realism, but as a significant fiction; and so he modestly and as it were playfully confesses his own authorship, for it is clear that the Duke is a figure of Shakespeare himself. It is a problem in the metaphysics or epistemology of poetry, like that which Dante solved in the *Divine Comedy* by speaking both as author and as protagonist; or like that which Pirandello explores in *Six Characters.*

It may be that Shakespeare solved this problem better in *The Tempest,* where, as G. Wilson Knight remarks, Prospero is lord of the play much as the Duke is in *Measure for Measure,* protagonist and author both. Prospero's art is presented, clearly, from the first, as magic, and that play may be regarded as a consistent though endlessly "true" fairy tale. In *Measure for Measure* Shakespeare's intention was different, perhaps more ambitious; he wished to go farther both in realism and in philosophic thought. If he succeeds, it can only be with a very alert and sophisticated audience.

Professor G. E. Bentley tells me that in his opinion *Measure for Measure* was not written for Shakespeare's usual popular audience, but for some special occasion. He thinks it possible, even probable, that it was written for the Inns of Court, though he adds that there is no real evidence for that. But I eagerly seize on this possibility, and I imagine Shakespeare himself, in the role of the Duke, addressing an audience professionally responsible for the Law. I see him in the Duke's costume, known for the theater man he was, speaking to his learned audience with urbanity and some irony:

> The properties of government to unfold
> Would seem, in me, to affect speech and discourse . . .

And after this polite gambit, I like to think of him enthralling the lawyers both with his philosophy of government and with the magic of his theater-poetry, lighting his great theme from several sides at once, yet passing it all off easily as his own hypothesis and make-believe.

Scenic Design in *Measure for Measure*

by *Anthony Caputi*

Much of the best criticism of *Measure for Measure* has focused on what one critic has called the "ethical pattern of the play." [1] Critics have by no means agreed on the nature of that pattern or its function, but an impressive number have agreed that the play is governed structurally by a conceptual scheme. The strength of this criticism derives from the fact that the play is unusually rich in ideas—particularly ideas about law and Christian doctrine. Yet to grant that these critics have properly identified the play's subject matter is not to accept their assumption about the play's structure: that an "ethical pattern" determines it, that a single or even multiple thesis about the law, Christian justice, mercy, or atonement can or ought to account for every detail of character, every placement of scene, and every fleeting allusion to the order of St. Clare.[2] Whatever its value, this approach to the play reveals an unmistakable weakness in its inability to deal with the total play without at some point invoking special responses dependent on a jurist's knowledge of Elizabethan law or elaborate theories of revision or textual corruption.

Indeed, something in the nature of this criticism has prevented a conclusive answer to the most basic question about the play: What

---

"Scenic Design in Measure for Measure*" by Anthony Caputi. From* Journal of English and Germanic Philology, *LX (1961), 423–34. Reprinted by permission of the University of Illinois Press and the author.*

[1] Elizabeth Marie Pope, "The Renaissance Background of *Measure for Measure*," *Shakespeare Survey*, II (1949), 78. [This article is included in this book—ED.] For a discussion of criticism to the present, see David L. Stevenson's "Design and Structure in *Measure for Measure*," *ELH* [*English Literary History*], XXIII (1956), 256–78.

[2] A sampling of such arguments can be found in M. C. Bradbrook's "Authority, Truth, and Justice in *Measure for Measure*," *RES* [*Review of English Studies*], XVII (1941), 385 ff., where she argues that the play takes the form of a "Contention between Justice and Mercy"; in R. W. Chambers' memorable "The Jacobean Shakespeare and *Measure for Measure*," *Proceedings of the British Academy*, XXIII (1937), 135–92 [an excerpt from the revision of this lecture is published in this book—ED.] where he describes it as a new-style Morality play designed to expound Christian forgiveness; and in Elizabeth Marie Pope's article, where she sees it as a carefully reasoned argument about the duties of a Christian ruler.

kind of play is *Measure for Measure?* Is it, as Hardin Craig insists, "gloomy and unpropitious"? Or is it, as R. W. Chambers argues, a paean to Christian forgiveness? Or is it, as one reviewer said of the recent production at the American Shakespeare Festival, "Lovely, rollicking, grand farce"? This question can probably never be answered with the certainty with which one might answer a similar question about a Plautine farce. Yet perhaps a fresh approach to the question can be undertaken if, while keeping what critics of the play's "ethical pattern" have said of its subject matter, we abandon their assumption about its structure and examine the play as a dramatic entity, one that achieves its peculiar power largely through a dramatic pattern. Such an approach inescapably emphasizes the large units from which the play is built rather than particular speeches, the general lines of development rather than nice points of theology and law. But in the process it directs attention to that dynamic unity so essential to a play's capacity to move an audience to a particular state of thought and feeling. And perhaps that is where the emphasis belongs.

Actually, the dramatic pattern of *Measure for Measure* is clearer than it might otherwise be, because of the rather clumsily joined seams that have prompted universal claims of textual corruption. This unfinished quality has left exposed an unusually clear outline of tensions and movement. Clues to this pattern are most easily found in two fairly obvious, if neglected, features of the play: Shakespeare's sporadic use of important characters and the dramatic design of certain scenes. In *Measure for Measure* Shakespeare has used his principal characters so irregularly as to imply unmistakably that character was not his primary concern. Angelo, for example, though extremely important early in the play, drops out of it between the end of Act II and IV. iv. The Duke, though he emerges in III. i to dominate the action, plays a rather slight part before Act III. Isabella, though a center of interest through III. i, becomes largely instrumental to the intrigue thereafter. And Mariana, though crucial to the action, is hardly prominent at all, indeed is not even mentioned until the end of III. i. The dramatic design encountered in key scenes is, perhaps, even more closely linked to the dramatic pattern that we are seeking to clarify. It is strange that so little has been made of the unusual design within scenes. Though the play has the usual five acts, almost three of them are given over to long scenes in which very little happens, scenes in which, instead of action, we get an inordinate amount of talk. After Act I, in which the action advances very rapidly, Act II settles down to a series of rather static interviews. First we have the long scene in which Escalus examines Pompey and Froth, then the long scene of Angelo's first interview with Isabella, then the short scene involving the Duke and Juliet, and then the long scene of

Angelo's second interview with Isabella. And the same is true of most of Act III. Only at the end of Act III does the action regain speed and variety to press into Act IV, where events move very rapidly. But in Act V the action again levels out, this time into one long trial scene.

Clearly any attempt to describe the structure of *Measure for Measure* must come to terms with these structural peculiarities. That they are what they are by intention seems beyond question: they are far too prominent to be the result of carelessness or a botched text. And that they are closely related to each other seems no less clear. It is altogether likely, in a play where great attention has been given to long, slowly developing scenes, often involving no more than two characters, that important characters will drop out of sight for long intervals. Thus Angelo does not appear from the end of Act II to the end of Act IV. He is a central character in his major scenes with Isabella, but almost irrelevant in Act III, where Claudio's interviews with the Duke and Isabella hold the stage. Thus the Duke appears only briefly in Act II, since here every resource is drawn upon to heighten the effect of Angelo's interviews with Isabella. And thus Isabella, after her big scenes in Acts II and III, becomes an instrumental character since interest subsequently centers in the Duke.

If we begin with the observation, then, that *Measure for Measure* gives unusual prominence to long, slowly developing scenes—indeed, that more than half of the play consists of such scenes—surely it would not be unreasonable to suppose that they contribute heavily to the play's power. An examination of these scenes reveals that all, with the notable exceptions of the short scene between the Duke and Claudio (III.i) and, for different reasons, the last act, are similar in structural outline in that all resemble informal debates or disputations.[3] Because they are conversational and spontaneous, they are, of course, different from the formal debate. But, like all debates, they typically involve two characters who articulate, carefully and at some length, *opposing positions.*

This feature alone has important implications for *Measure for Measure.* Clearly, in scenes wherein characters argue something at length, as compared with scenes—like the banquet scene in *Macbeth*—in which events develop rapidly and unexpectedly, the dual effect is that they draw the audience's critical faculty into play and insist upon a certain critical distance. But this feature, if pressed further, leads to still more important observations. If we compare the scenes in question (excepting, again, the Duke's scene with Claudio and the last act), we discover that in none of them are the opposing positions reconciled. On the contrary, all end in unresolved states of conflict:

---

[3] Bradbrook develops this point at some length, pp. 385-95.

characters meet, talk, discover differences of opinion, discuss their differences, and part only after having heightened the tension expressed by their disagreement. Moreover, if we compare the opposing positions expressed in these scenes, we also find a certain consistency among them. In each the conflict involves one character who takes, essentially, the position of civilized man with confidence in his codes and decorums, and a second character who takes, essentially, the position of natural man with a vivid sense of his frailties and imperfections. In II.i, Escalus speaks for civilization and Pompey for the "poor fellow that would live"; in II.ii, Angelo defends the law while Isabella defends natural man against it; in II.iv, Angelo and Isabella change roles; and, subsequently, Claudio, the Duke, and Lucio take their turns. As the argument develops and the positions crystallize, they become increasingly irreconcilable. We are made distinctly aware that the positions taken by the characters are drawing apart until, at the end of each scene, the situation seems hopelessly stalemated—far worse than it was at the beginning.

Of course even this general description requires some qualification. However stalemated Escalus and Pompey seem at the end of their scene, obviously their scene is qualitatively very different from Angelo's scene with Isabella. By setting aside the low-life scenes for a moment, however, we can see that all the other pertinent scenes are designed to convey a vivid impression of the incompatibility of civilized and natural man, to bring before us in almost paradigm form a dramatized challenge to civilized or moral life. By communicating an awareness of the inadequacy of law and decorum to man's condition and, conversely, an awareness of man's inadequacy to his laws and codes, these scenes generate a disturbing sense of the very precarious foundations on which civilized life is built—what, for the purposes of this play, can be called a distinct sense of moral distress.

In view of the prominence of these scenes in the first three acts and of the qualitatively comparable scene in Act IV, in which the Duke waits for Claudio's pardon only to learn that Angelo is capable of depths he dreamed not of, we can tentatively infer that the dramatic pattern of the first four acts of *Measure for Measure* is calculated to make us feel much of what the Duke feels in III.ii, that "there is scarce truth enough alive to make societies secure, but security enough to make fellowships accursed: much upon this riddle runs the wisdom of the world" (ll. 219–22). This speech offers the play's most explicit statement about the represented condition of civilized life, the most direct glance at the disparity between what man fondly aspires to and what he is. To support this description of the play's power in more detail, however, we must go back to the scenes that dramatize this perception, and particularly to the details of design within scenes that control the sense of moral distress. We can then consider how the last act is designed to dispel it.

It is relevant, first, to look at two conspicuous loose ends in the pattern thus far described. The long scene involving Escalus, Froth, and Pompey in II.i plainly dramatizes the typical conflicting positions and plainly shows them to be irreconcilable; but surely we do not respond to this scene with anything like distress. And if we say that the famous scene between the Duke and Claudio generates a sense of distress, we must admit that in this instance the distress does not proceed from marked disagreement. However consistent with the dramatic pattern thus far discerned, these scenes also deviate from it; and they deviate with good purpose.

The structural analogy between the Escalus-Pompey scene and the other interview scenes provides an important insight into the function of the low-life characters in the play. Actually, the analogy is hardly limited to this scene: throughout the play Pompey, Mistress Overdone, and Barnardine are at odds with law and morality. In other words, throughout the play they dramatize a conflict like that dramatized rather painfully in the scenes involving Angelo, Isabella, Claudio, and the Duke. Yet certainly we do not respond to the conflict as they dramatize it with feelings any more serious than a sense of exhilarating incongruity, perhaps even of exhilarating futility. By and large, we are in sympathy with what they represent, however much we may resent it. They are the eternal yardbirds of civilized life, who, like Pompey Bum, will always muddle through to the easiest jobs—even in prison. They represent the intractability of human nature: its refusal to submit to laws and codes, indeed, in the case of Barnardine, its contemptuous defiance of them. Moreover, these low-life offenders have their counterpart among the representatives of law and order: Elbow, with his genius for getting things wrong side to, is unmistakably a comic variation on Escalus and Angelo. The scenes involving these characters provide a comic exhibition of the precariousness of civilized foundations that counterpoints the more serious dramatization of the other scenes. They furnish a kind of comic obbligato that prevents the feelings of distress aroused from becoming too intense, and tempers these feelings with complexity of outlook. To put the matter another way, the low-life scenes control the quality of the other interview scenes by putting them in a framework that adds comic dimensions to otherwise serious exhibitions of moral disorder; they dramatize what must always be funny from the detached point of view of the comic muse: the hilarity of man's high designs.

The Duke's great scene with Claudio, on the other hand, is nothing if not serious. Traditionally, it has given critics trouble because it is

almost too serious, because it expresses so gloomy a view of life as to
be out of keeping with the long-range optimism of the Christian doctrine everywhere in evidence. But the scene also poses difficulties of
a much less subtle kind. At this point in the play we have no evidence
that Claudio, who has not appeared since Act I, will not face death
courageously; and though we find it normal that a friar would con-
sole a condemned man, we are surprised to learn that so impressive
a consolation comes to nought in the next scene, where Claudio seems
to have forgotten everything the Duke as friar has said. Perhaps the
first point to be made about this scene, accordingly, is that it has a
very slight function in the chain of episodes: it in no significant way
advances the action. Its function, rather, seems to be to intensify the
peculiar power of the scenes immediately preceding and following it.
Coming just after Isabella's scenes with Angelo and just before her
scene with Claudio, this scene, and especially the Duke's elaborate
consolation, serve chiefly to focus the energies generated up to this
point, to heighten the play's pervasive sense of the insecurity of human
affairs.

> Reason thus with life:
> If I do lose thee, I do lose a thing
> That none but fools would keep: a breath thou art,
> Servile to all the skyey influences,
> . . . Merely, thou art death's fool,
> . . . Thou art not noble,
> . . . Thou'rt by no means valiant,
> . . . Thou art not thyself,
> . . . Happy thou art not,
> . . . Thou art not certain,
> . . . If thou art rich, thou'rt poor,
> . . . Friend hast thou none,
> . . . Thou has nor youth nor age,
> But as it were an after-dinner's sleep,
> Dreaming on both . . .
> . . . and when thou art old and rich,
> Thou hast neither heat, affection, limb, nor beauty,
> To make thy riches pleasant. What's yet in this,
> That bears the name of life? Yet in this life
> Lie hid moe thousand deaths; yet death we fear,
> That makes these odds all even.   (III.i. 6–41)

This is not a tragic perception of insecurity, qualified, as it is, by the
low-life characters and seen, as it is, with considerable detachment.
But it is the dominant perception, and one that emphasizes the detached sobriety rather than the gaiety of comedy.

In our inspection of other scenes, we need not deal here with the short scenes, like those met chiefly in Acts I and IV. They clearly have the main function of laying down the probabilities of action and character necessary to support the play's big scenes. Scenes as important as those involving Angelo and Isabella in Act II, however, require detailed examination. Both characters have prompted considerable comment, and perhaps no Shakespearean character has occasioned so much disagreement as Isabella. The traditional alternatives for her—that she is either an exalted ideal or a travesty on womanhood—seem violently extreme and dangerously simple. It is probable that Shakespeare's contemporaries found much to admire in her intensity of purpose, her quickness of mind and aptness of tongue, and her courage. It is doubtful, however, that even they were meant to warm to her decision to save her chastity by permitting her brother to die. On the contrary, apparently Shakespeare has consciously forced this dreadful choice on her—dreadful because neither alternative is satisfactory—and, in order to scale down her attractiveness somewhat, has made her put this choice in unusually cold, succinct, almost painfully simple terms.

> Better it were a brother died at once,
> Than a sister, by redeeming him,
> Should die forever.   (II.iv. 106–108)

> Then Isabel live chaste, and brother die;
> More than our brother is our chastity.
>   (II.iv. 184–85)

>   Dost thou think, Claudio?
> If I would yield him my virginity,
> Thou mightst be freed.   (III.i. 96–98)

Unquestionably, Shakespeare has very carefully scaled her down in other ways. Lucio's speeches in I.iv and II.ii help to adjust our attitude toward her. In the nunnery scene (I.iv) he begins with a parody, "Hail, virgin," and continues with tongue in cheek. Despite all attempts to read his praise of her literally ("I hold you as a thing enskied and sainted"), there is nothing in his character or in his subsequent description of her to justify the reading. Obviously, he does not fool Isabella, who replies, "You do blaspheme the good, in mocking me" (l. 38). Then later, during Isabella's first interview with Angelo (II.ii), Lucio's remarks, "You are too cold" (ll.45, 56), serve unmistakably to underline this shortcoming in her. For all Isabella's admirable qualities, the truth is that she is out of her element in the world of Lucio, Angelo, and even Claudio. Her most stirring quality is the cold fire she suggests when arguing law and morality. Though we view her with sympathy and admiration, we do so with considerable detachment.

Angelo is a far simpler matter than Isabella. In Acts I and II we have every reason to believe reports that he is a man of strictest virtue. Indeed, Shakespeare carefully withholds all information about Mariana until late in III.i, so that we may believe these reports. In Act II we see him take a position on the question of Claudio and withstand firmly the successive assaults made on it by Escalus (II.i), the Provost (II.ii), and Isabella (II.ii). Up to this moment he is a kind of abstract extreme, a point of view with respect to the problems that have developed. After he has succumbed to Isabella's physical attractions, he is the only character whom we know through introspective soliloquies. (The Duke speaks soliloquies, but they consist of choral comments on the state of society.) Yet even this interest in Angelo's character is very carefully controlled: just when he is becoming most interesting, he drops out of the play for almost two acts, and our attention is whisked away to Claudio, Isabella, the Duke, and Mariana. Like Isabella, he is distinctly subordinate to a larger design that invites us to view him with fascination, but with a fairly detached, critical fascination.[4]

When Isabella appears before Angelo in II.ii, both characters represent extremes: Isabella is as much as possible like a nun without actually being one, and Angelo (partly because Shakespeare has withheld all information about Mariana) is very like a monk. In this juxtaposition alone consists a great deal of the interest of this and their second interview, especially when toward the end of this scene their relations take so sensational a turn. The structural interest of the scene lies in the development of the conflict between them, a development that Lucio and the Provost very carefully accentuate. At the beginning of II.ii, Isabella takes the most difficult of positions for one pleading for Claudio's life: she admits that she hates Claudio's sin to the point of being reluctant to plead for him. Angelo, on the other hand, takes a position that even at the outset seems impregnable: he implies that he could do something, but he "will not do't" (l. 57). With these positions established, much of the suspense of the scene proceeds from the attempts to reconcile them. We hope that Isabella will win Angelo over; but she is only half-hearted and he immovable. Only gradually does she catch fire, and then, as she drives narrow wedges into his argument and their positions seem to draw together, the scene builds to the shocking disclosure that she has succeeded only in arousing his desire for her. This sensational turn throws open a whole new set of possibilities, and in the second inter-

---

[4] See Stevenson, pp. 262–64, for another approach to this feature of the play.

view Angelo and Isabella take entirely new positions, though every
bit as irreconcilable as the first.

The second interview builds in much the same way, but rests on
different devices. Here the suspense is produced and sustained first
by Isabella's apparent failure to understand Angelo's proposal. When
she has understood it and rejected it, tension continues to mount as
he becomes firmer and finds that he can charge her with inconsistency,
while she attacks him, with increasing heat, for baseness. The ac-
celeration of tempo and excitement is again, we should notice, correspondent to the intensifying antagonism between the points of view
represented. At the end of the scene we are aware not only that they
are farther apart than before, but also that there seems to be no
satisfactory compromise for the conflict they have dramatized.

Following the next scene—the interview between the Duke and
Claudio—the scene between Isabella and Claudio is in structure and
effect very like the Angelo-Isabella interviews. Here the suspense is
sustained by Isabella's reluctance to reveal Angelo's proposal and her
decision. At this point she serves to develop in the audience a new
apprehensiveness, in that she, too, has had her confidence shaken: she
has come to fear for Claudio's sense of honor, for the genuineness of
his commitment as a civilized man. Yet despite all her caution, the
characteristic disparity of positions develops, to emerge clear in Claudio's declaration that "Death is a fearful thing" (l. 115).

Taken as a group, these scenes trace the dominant dramatic pattern
of the first two-thirds of the play, and lead to the explicit impasse of
the scene in Act IV where the Duke's first plan is upset by Angelo
(IV.ii). In the main they convey a distinct perception of the flimsiness
of civilized life: of the distressing inadequacy of man's efforts at civilization and of the comic incongruity of his pretensions to it. But our
description of the play's dramatic pattern is hardly complete until we
consider the Duke's role in all this, and the ways in which the long
final scene dispels this serio-comic distress.

The Duke's role is sufficiently important to consider at some length.
After his brief appearances in Acts I and II, he emerges in III.i to
dominate the action. Thereafter, he is either eavesdropping from
some dark corner or deliberately ordering events: making arrange-
ments with Isabella, Mariana, the Provost, and Friar Peter. To see
the importance of his presence in the scenes from III.i to the end, we
need only consider what we know because of his disguise that the
characters in the play, except for Friar Peter, do not know. Most
significantly, we know that the Duke *is* in disguise, that he is observ-
ing everything, and that he is capable at any moment of averting dis-
aster. Surely the chief result of this knowledge is our confidence that
Angelo cannot succeed, that the action is destined for a favorable

outcome. The Duke's disguise, then, serves chiefly to control the sense of distress aroused and to lead, with probability, to its dispersion in the last act. After his emergence in III.i, this sense of distress gradually diminishes as he takes an increasingly prominent hand in the action. As we are assured that he intends to avert catastrophe, our awareness of moral disorder gradually gives way to an awareness that the characters perceive moral disorder where, in fact, it does not have absolute sway. The emergence of this reassurance is very carefully controlled—particularly through the Duke—until in the last act the machinery of the plot is thrown into reverse: where in the first four acts the characters have continually met with worse developments than they—or we—have expected, in the last act they continually meet with better.

A corollary function of the Duke's disguise is that it also diminishes the long-range melodramatic suspense that could have proceeded from these otherwise very melodramatic scenes in favor of fixing our attention on the moral quality of the action. Suspense in this play is not built on such questions as "How will this turn out?" Because of the Duke, we know or, at least, are reasonably certain about how it will turn out. Instead, we are invited to attend closely and critically to what is happening at the moment in scenes contrived to generate a short-range suspense of their own. The Duke's disguise, accordingly, is yet another part of the general pattern calculated to encourage us to view the separate events of the play critically.

Having quietly rearranged everything to his satisfaction, the Duke simply sits back in Act V to let the intrigue work itself out. Clearly the primary function of Act V is to cause our sense of distress to yield to a sense of reassurance, to supplement our perception of the precariousness of civilized foundations with the perception that with understanding man can regulate, if not remedy, his difficult situation; indeed, he can occasionally achieve the poetic justice that the Duke in his temporary omniscience manages at the end of the play. It is, finally, a sense of assurance that, however precarious the foundations of civilized life, man will somehow sustain it.

This reassurance proceeds from the last act in a number of ways, some of which involve solid evidence for it, others of which are little more than artifice. To begin with, it proceeds from the reversed pattern of developments already mentioned. More important, and more conspicuously, it proceeds from the leisurely exposure and punishment of Angelo and even of Lucio. If the last act is long for any reason, it is because the Duke is so unhurried about exposing Angelo. Instead of denouncing him immediately, as well he might, he permits him to extend himself as completely as possible. And after he has exposed him, he prolongs his anguish by permitting him to believe that he is to die for Claudio's death. This leisureliness is important. To relieve the intense antipathy that has been built up against Angelo and still conclude the play with forgiveness for him, Shakespeare had to dramatize his punishment. To do this, he had to entangle Angelo so profoundly in the Duke's web that at the moment of the Duke's unhooding Angelo disgraces himself publicly and completely. At this moment, Angelo's overwhelming sense of failure is almost adequate to expiate the crimes that he actually succeeded in committing.

Lucio, on the other hand, is a rather different matter. As many have observed, he is something of a scapegoat in the sense that, though he deserves his punishment, it seems in part contrived to relieve feelings of righteous indignation aroused in other quarters. However true this may be, Lucio serves chiefly at this point to support our growing assurance of the efficacy of law, not only by providing the Duke with an occasion to exercise it, but partly by providing him an opportunity to identify and punish its most serious enemy in the play. For all Lucio's lightheartedness, his is in many ways the low point of cynicism in the play: unlike Pompey and Barnardine, he is a man in whom we expect beliefs; yet he has none. He has no serious loyalties and no capacity for guilt or repentance because he is incapable of a serious commitment of any kind. There is, accordingly, a subtle justice in the Duke's active disapproval of him that has very little to do with the Duke's personal pique. In one sense Lucio's punishment represents the finest adjustment, though hardly the most important, that the just forces make toward the end of the play.

At any rate, the length of this final act is necessary to strengthen the sense of confidence and assurance we have felt all through it so that these feelings are sufficiently strong to be dominant at the end. The marriages serve simply to support these feelings. That they do not produce the rejoicing produced by an *As You Like It* means no more than that Shakespeare did not intend them to. *Measure for Measure* is, throughout, a play in which our concern about the characters' fortunes is distinctly subordinate to our concern about the fortunes of civilization. It is civilization as it is at issue in the careers of Isabella, Claudio, Angelo, the Duke, Pompey, Barnardine, and others that chiefly enlists our attention and engages our feelings.

It is doubtless for this reason that so many critics have been drawn to an abstract analysis of the play's ideas. No one would deny that the play abounds in ideas. But however important, they do not alter the fact that, no less than *King Lear* or *Twelfth Night*, *Measure for Measure* is, structurally, a dramatic rather than an intellectual persuasion and that, as such, its capacity to move an audience to an enlightened state of feelings depends largely on the direction and control of its dramatic pattern. It is only this kind of pattern that can put the marriages at the end in a reasonable perspective, a perspective in which they are not required to complete a conceptual formulation, but serve quite simply and effectively to support the affirmation of faith in civilization on which the play closes. By viewing the play from this point of view we do not solve all problems, it is true, but we do eliminate many pseudo-problems by making dramatic sense of a play that never asked to be a dark intellectual puzzle.

Measure for Measure

by E. M. W. Tillyard

The simple and ineluctable fact is that the tone in the first half of the play is frankly, acutely human and quite hostile to the tone of allegory or symbol. And, however much the tone changes in the second half, nothing in the world can make an allegorical interpretation poetically valid throughout.

Recent critics, in their anxiety to correct old errors, have in fact gone too far in the other direction and ignored one of the prime facts from which those old errors had their origin: namely that the play is not of a piece but changes its nature half-way through. It was partly through their correct perception of something being wrong that some earlier critics felt justified in making the Isabella of the first half of the play the scapegoat of the play's imperfections.

The above inconsistency has long been noted, but since of late it has been so strongly denied, I had better assert it once more, and if possible not quite in the old terms. Briefly, the inconsistency is the most serious and complete possible, being one of literary style. Up to III. 1. 151, when the Duke enters to interrupt the passionate conversation between Claudio and Isabella on the conflicting claims of his life and her chastity, the play is predominantly poetical, the poetry being, it is true, set off by passages of animated prose. And the poetry is of that kind of which Shakespeare is the great master, the kind that seems extremely close to the business of living, to the problem of how to function as a human being. One character after another is pictured in a difficult, a critical, position, and yet one which all of us can imagine ourselves to share; and the poetry answers magnificently to this penetrating sense of human intimacy. Up to the above point the Duke, far from being guide and controller, has been a mere conventional piece of dramatic convenience for creating the setting for the human conflicts. Beyond that he is just an onlooker. And, as

"Measure for Measure" by E. M. W. Tillyard. From Shakespeare's Problem Plays *(London: Chatto & Windus Ltd., 1950; Toronto: University of Toronto Press, 1950), pp. 123–29. Reprinted by permission of Mrs. Veronica Sankaran and the publishers.*

pointed out above, any symbolic potentialities the characters may possess are obscured by the tumult of passions their minds present to us. From the Duke's entry at III. 1. 151 to the end of the play there is little poetry of any kind and scarcely any of the kind described above. There is a passage of beautiful verse spoken by the Provost, Claudio, and the Duke in the prison, IV. 2. 66 ff. Take these lines from it:

> Prov.   It is a bitter deputy.
> Duke. Not so, not so: his life is parallel'd
>   Even with the stroke and line of his great justice.
>   He doth with holy abstinence subdue
>   That in himself which he spurs on his power
>   To qualify in others. Were he meal'd with that
>   Which he corrects, then were he tyrannous;
>   But this being so, he's just.

In their way these lines cannot be bettered but they do not touch the great things in the early part of the play; their accent is altogether more subdued. Again, the episode of Mariana and Isabella pleading to the Duke for Angelo's life, in the last scene of all, does rise somewhat as poetry. But this exceptional passage counts for little in the prevailing tone of lowered poetical tension. Where in the first half the most intense writing was poetical, in the second half it is comic or at least prosaic. While the elaborate last scene, as I have already pointed out, for all its poetical pretensions is either a dramatic failure or at best a Pyrrhic victory, it is the comedy of Lucio and the Duke, of Pompey learning the mystery of the executioner from Abhorson, of Barnardine (for Shakespeare somehow contrives to keep his gruesomeness this side the comic) that makes the second half of the play possible to present on the stage with any success at all. And the vehicle of this comedy is prose, which, excellent though it is, cannot be held consistent with the high poetry of the first half. Another evident sign of tension relaxed in the second half of the play is the increased use of rhyme. Not that it occurs in such long stretches as in All's Well; but there are many short passages, like this soliloquy of the Duke after hearing Lucio's scandalous remarks on his character in III. 2:

> No might nor greatness in mortality
> Can censure 'scape; back-wounding calumny
> The whitest virtue strikes. What king so strong
> Can tie the gall up in the sland'rous tongue?

or the couplet containing the title of the play:

> Haste still pays haste, and leisure answers leisure;
> Like doth quit like, and Measure still for Measure.

Here an antique quaintness excuses the lack of poetic intensity. Most characteristic of this quality in the last half of the play are the Duke's octosyllabic couplets at the end of III. 2:

> He who the sword of heaven will bear
> Should be as holy as severe:
> Pattern in himself to know,
> Grace to stand, and virtue go;
> More nor less to others paying
> Than by self-offences weighing—

and the rest. Far from being spurious, the Duke's couplets in their antique stiffness and formality agree with the whole trend of the play's second half in relaxing the poetical tension and preparing for a more abstract form of drama.

A similar inconsistency extends to some of the characters. From being a minor character in the first half, with no influence on the way human motives are presented, the Duke becomes the dominant character in the second half and the one through whose mind human motives are judged. In the first half of the play we are in the very thick of action, where different human beings have their own special and different problems and are concerned with how to settle them. Mistress Overdone's problem of what's to be done now all the houses of resort in the suburbs are to be pulled down stands on its own feet quite separate from Claudio's problem of what's to be done now he has been arrested. We are in fact too close to them both to be able to distance them into a single perspective or a common unifying colour. Reality is too urgent to allow of reflection. In the second half the Duke is in charge. He has his plans, and, knowing they will come to fruition, we can watch their workings. Reflection has encroached on reality. W. W. Lawrence wrote a fine chapter on *Measure for Measure,* in which he points to the Duke's multifarious functions. The Duke's part derives both from the old folk-motive of the sovereign in disguise mixing with his people and from the conventional stage-character of the plot-promoting priest. He combines the functions of church and state. In his disguise he "represents the wisdom and adroitness of the Church in directing courses of action and advising stratagems so that good may come out of evil." He is also the supreme ruler of Vienna who at the end "straightens out the tangles of the action and dispenses justice to all." He is also a stage figure, highly important for manipulating the action and contrasted strikingly with the realistic characters. Admitting most truly that "Shakespeare's art oscillates between extreme psychological subtlety and an equally extreme disregard of psychological truth, in the acceptance of stock narrative conventions," Lawrence may imply that the Duke does succeed in uniting these extremes. If so, I can only disagree, because Lawrence's description of the Duke applies only faintly to the first half of the play.

Nowhere does the change in the Duke's position show so strikingly as in Isabella. There is no more independent character in Shakespeare than the Isabella of the first half of the play: and independent in two senses. The essence of her disposition is decision and the acute sense of her own independent and inviolate personality; while her own particular problem of how to act is presented with all that differentiation which I attributed to the problems of Claudio and Mistress Overdone. At the beginning of the third act, when she has learnt Angelo's full villainy, her nature is working at the very height of its accustomed freedom. She enters almost choked with bitter fury at Angelo, in the mood for martyrdom and feeling that Claudio's mere life is a trifle before the mighty issues of right and wrong. Her scorn of Claudio's weakness is dramatically definitive and perfect. To his pathetic pleas, "Sweet sister, let me live" etc., the lines Scott prefixed to the twentieth chapter of the *Heart of Midlothian,* comes, as it must, her own, spontaneous retort from the depth of her being,

> O you beast,
> O faithless coward, O dishonest wretch!
> Wilt thou be made a man out of my vice?
> Is't not a kind of incest to take life
> From thine own sister's shame? What should I think?
> Heaven shield my mother play'd my father fair,
> For such a warped slip of wilderness
> Ne'er issued from his blood. Take my defiance,
> Die, perish! Might but my bending down
> Reprieve thee from thy fate, it should proceed.
> I'll pray a thousand prayers for thy death,
> No word to save thee.

That is the true Isabella, and whether or not we like that kind of woman is beside the point. But immediately after her speech, at line 152, the Duke takes charge and she proceeds to exchange her native ferocity for the hushed and submissive tones of a well-trained confidential secretary. To the Duke's inquiry of how she will content Angelo and save her brother she replies in coolly rhetorical prose:

I am now going to resolve him: I had rather my brother die by the law than my son should be unlawfully born. But, O, how much is the good duke deceived in Angelo! If ever he return and I can speak to him, I will open my lips in vain or discover his government.

But such coolness is warm compared with her tame acquiescence in the Duke's plan for her to pretend to yield to Angelo and then to substitute Mariana:

> The image of it gives me content already, and I trust it will grow to a most prosperous perfection.

To argue, as has been argued, that the plan, by Elizabethan standards, was very honourable and sensible and that of course Isabella would have accepted it gladly is to substitute the criterion of ordinary practical common sense for that of the drama. You could just as well seek to compromise the fictional validity of Jeanie Deans's journey to London by proving that the initial practical difficulties of such a journey at such a date rendered the undertaking highly improbable. In Scott's novel Jeanie Deans does travel to London, and, though Scott had better have shorn her journey of many of its improbable and romantic complications, it is a consistent Jeanie Deans who takes the journey, and her action in taking the journey and in pleading with the Queen is significant. Isabella, on the contrary, has been bereft of significant action, she has nothing to do corresponding to Jeanie's journey, and she has turned into a mere tool of the Duke. In the last scene she does indeed bear some part in the action; but her freedom of utterance is so hampered by misunderstanding and mystification that she never speaks with her full voice: she is not, dramatically, the same Isabella. That the Duke is in his way impressive, that he creates a certain moral atmosphere, serious and yet tolerant, in the second half of the play need not be denied; yet that atmosphere can ill bear comparison with that of the early part of the play. To this fact Lucio is the chief witness. He is now the livest figure and the one who does most to keep the play from quite falling apart, and he almost eludes the Duke's control. He is as it were a minor Saturnian deity who has somehow survived into the iron age of Jupiter; and a constant reminder that the Saturnian age was the better of the two.

PART THREE

View Points

William Witherle Lawrence: The Duke

The ruler of the degenerate city of Vienna is, I believe, to be regarded as a conventional and romantic figure, whose actions are mainly determined by theatrical exigencies and effectiveness; he is, as it were, a stage Duke, not a real person. In this respect he contrasts strikingly with Isabella and Angelo and Claudio and Lucio, and the low-comedy people. Most of the misunderstandings of his part in the play have been due to failure to perceive this. Nothing shows more vividly the conventional elements in Shakespeare's technique than an analysis of the Duke's varied activities.

In the dramas written before *Measure for Measure,* two agencies stand out prominently as representatives of right and justice in straightening out complications of plot: the State and the Church. The former is represented by the person in supreme lay authority—a Duke in the *Comedy of Errors,* the *Two Gentlemen of Verona, Twelfth Night,* the *Midsummer Night's Dream* (Theseus as Duke of Athens), the *Merchant of Venice, As You Like It* (the Banished Duke); the King of France in *All's Well.* The latter is represented by priest or friar—Friar Laurence in *Romeo and Juliet,* Friar Francis in *Much Ado,* who suggest, respectively, the stratagems by which the Veronese lovers are united, and the honor of Hero vindicated. The law and authority in these pieces is romantic law and authority; it cannot be judged by strict legal or ecclesiastical standards. The quibbles which are the undoing of Shylock are as much a part of popular story as the sleeping potion which sends Juliet to the tomb. Shakespeare used dukes and friars when the peculiar powers and opportunities afforded by their station would help his narrative. He did not bother himself about the strict legality or rationality of their actions. What they suggest or decide has in his plays the binding force of constituted and final authority, and was so understood by his audiences.

The Duke in *Measure for Measure* combines the functions both of State and Church in his person. As Duke, he is supreme ruler of

"The Duke" by William Witherle Lawrence. From "Measure for Measure" *in* Shakespeare's Problem Comedies *(New York: The Macmillan Company, 1931; 2nd edn., Frederick Ungar Publishing Co., 1960), pp. 102–4. Copyright © 1960 by Frederick Ungar Publishing Co. Reprinted by permission of the publisher.*

Vienna, who returns at the end to straighten out the tangles of the action, and dispense justice to all. In his disguise as Friar, he represents the wisdom and adroitness of the Church, in directing courses of action and advising stratagems so that good may come out of evil. But the plots which he sets in motion and the justice which he dispenses are the stuff of story; they cannot be judged as if they were historical occurrences. And the Duke's character cannot be estimated on a rationalistic basis. If he really wished to set matters right between Angelo, Isabella, Mariana, Claudio, and the rest, he had a short and easy way of doing it. He was in full possession of the facts; he could have revealed himself, brought all before the bar of his authority, freed the innocent and punished the guilty in short order, and this would have saved Isabella and Claudio much suffering. Such an arrangement would, however, have been much less effective dramatically than his continued disguise, his suggested ruses, the prolongation of the suspense of the accused and the false security of the villain. No, he knows what is expected of him as a stage Duke, and makes the most of his part.

Murray Krieger: Measure for Measure *and Elizabethan Comedy*

It should be clear that the two lines of Elizabethan comedy we have traced are completely opposed to each other.* In addition to their different attitudes toward such superficial structural principles as the three unities, there are two antithetical concepts of drama involved here. In one there is the primacy of character-consistency, in the other the primacy of fanciful plot. In one, no perilous element is allowed to obfuscate the purely comic effect; in the other even the most tragic possibilities may enter along the way, provided that all ends well. One demands from its audience an attitude of detachment, of disdainful superiority; the other demands so sympathetic a concern for the fortunes of its characters that the audience will tolerate anything so long as the obstacles to a happy ending are cleared away. While Shakespeare's comedies are commonly of the romantic variety and therefore close to Greene's, it must not be forgotten that the "humorous" comedies of Jonson, only recently originated, had attained great popularity by the time Shakespeare came to write *Measure for Measure*

"Measure for Measure *and Elizabethan Comedy" by Murray Krieger. From* Publications of the Modern Language Association of America, *LXVI (1951), 781–83. Reprinted by permission of The Modern Language Association of America.*
* [A reference to "Classical" and "Romantic" comedy.—Ed.]

and his other so-called "dark comedies." And this new fashion may have been the influence which forced these comedies to be so different from his earlier ones.

It seems likely that the two conflicting varieties of Elizabethan comedy, that of Jonson and that of Greene, are combined in *Measure for Measure,* and that their incompatibility has caused the critical confusion which still exists about the play. Recognizing this duality, we also, like most of the commentators discussed earlier, would see the play as having two incongruous elements, but these would not be so easily separated at any one point in the action as they would have us believe. Rather Shakespeare seems to be doing two things at once throughout this work. Campbell, in his *Shakespeare's Satire,* has carefully examined the play in terms of the elements in it of the comedy of ridicule. He concludes, however, that the play fails because Isabella, who structurally is the Duke's device to gull Angelo, outgrows her function and, in outgrowing it, threatens to become the heroine of a serious play. It should be added to this analysis, I believe, that Isabella's development is not so much an accident or loss of control during playwriting as it is a manifestation of a clearly defined variety of romantic comedy which had its hold on Shakespeare and which he could not or would not shake off even as he was introducing the currently popular Jonsonian characteristics. As a result, he tried to graft the latter elements on to the fundamentally different tradition of comedy to which he formerly was devoted, but failed to blend the two. Perhaps the two concepts, being too opposed, inevitably involved too many incongruities to allow an organic union or, for that matter, to allow anything more than an unintegrated superimposition of one on the other. Be that as it may, it is important, in returning to Isabella, that we see how she is shaped by both traditions. In addition to and simultaneously with the conventional satiric function attributed to her by Campbell, Isabella, as the supremely virtuous woman whose purity is threatened by a vicious ruler, is called upon to function as an equally conventional counterpart of Greene's heroines. Using Campbell's Jonsonian analysis on the one hand, but supplementing it continually by considering the influence of this other kind of comedy, we should see into the ambiguity of many key situations and characters in the play.

In light of Campbell's presentation and in view of the fact that there are no pastoral elements as such in the play, one may say that *Measure for Measure* is farther from Greene and closer to Jonson than are Shakespeare's earlier and more obviously romantic comedies. Nevertheless it is also evident that his earlier romantic characteristics are there constantly to battle the classical ones for supremacy. For example, the puritanical Angelo, Campbell states, is the Jonsonian gull, and the entire play is so constructed as to expose his hidden vices. On the face of it, this would indeed seem to differentiate him from Shylock or Don John, who are the purely romantic villains. But it must be noted on the other side that his vices take on a far more serious aspect than Jonson would permit, and that in this respect he shows a close resemblance to the Scotch king in *James IV*, as well as to Shylock and Don John. Consequently, at the same time as he is the gull, he is the conventional villain of romantic comedy whose defeat is necessary. And his final repentance has a similar duality about it. On the one hand there is evidence that he is purged of his vice in Jonsonian fashion; on the other hand he appears to undergo the unforeseen and unjustifiable change-of-heart that is characteristic of a comedy by Greene or an earlier one by Shakespeare.

If we add to this analysis of Angelo's role the ambiguous function of Isabella as romantic heroine and as tool for the Duke's plot—a point which has already been touched upon—the contradictory character of the play becomes clear. Seen in this light, the play reveals how complete a struggle it is between the two opposed patterns of comedy. The one has Angelo as the main character and gull, with Isabella as the means of gulling him (and would not Jonson rather use a courtesan, the classic functional type?). The other is a story of romantic adventure presenting Isabella as the pure heroine and Angelo as the lustful villain who repents after he is overcome. And, as we have seen, our emotional response can hardly cope with such divergent demands. By studying the play in terms of the framework suggested here, we can also account for the many critical objections to Isabella's moral consistency. True to her romantic counterparts, she must withstand Angelo's advances at all costs and rebuke Claudio for pleading that she yield herself in order to save him. But as the instrument of Jonsonian intrigue, she must turn around and engineer the Mariana "bed trick." Thus the inconsistency of the play, as well as the difficulty of critics with it, does not, as it is commonly claimed, spring from a confusion of moral principles so much as it springs from a confusion of two technical patterns, each of which makes different moral demands. At their source, then, the problems are revealed as formal rather than thematic.

R. W. Chambers: Isabella Approved

If we fail to see the nobility of Isabel, we cannot see the story as we should. The plot is rather like that of Calderon's *Magician,*

"Isabella Approved" (original title: "Measure for Measure") by R. W. Chambers.

where the scholarly, austere Cipriano is overthrown by speaking with the saintly Justina. Cipriano sells himself literally to the Devil to gain his end by magic. Angelo tempts Isabel in a second dialogue, as wonderful as the first. In her innocence Isabel is slow to see Angelo's drift, and it is only her confession of her own frailty that gives him a chance of making himself clear. "Nay," Isabel says,

> call us ten times frail;
> For we are soft as our complexions are,
> And credulous to false prints.

If Shakespeare is depicting in Isabel the self-righteous prude which some critics would make of her, he goes strangely to work.

But when she perceives Angelo's meaning, Isabel decides without hesitation. Now whatever we think of that instant decision, it is certainly not un-Christian. Christianity could never have lived through its first three hundred years of persecution, if its ranks had not been stiffened by men and women who never hesitated in the choice between righteousness and the ties to their kinsfolk. We may call this fanaticism: but it was well understood in Shakespeare's day. Foxe's *Martyrs* was read by all; old people could still remember seeing the Smithfield fires; year after year saw the martyrdoms of Catholic men (and sometimes of Catholic women like the Ven. Margaret Clitherow). It was a stern age—an age such as the founder of Christianity had foreseen when he uttered his stern warnings. "He that loveth father or mother more than me . . ." "If any man come to me, and hate not his father, and mother, . . . and brethren and sisters, . . . he cannot be my disciple." [1]

It is recorded of Linacre, the father of English medicine, that, albeit a priest, he opened his Greek New Testament for the first time late in life, and came on some of these hard sayings. "Either this is not the Gospel," he said, "or we are not Christians," and refusing to contemplate the second alternative, he flung the Book from him and returned to the study of medicine. Now it is open to us to say that we are not Christians: it is not open to us to say that Isabel is un-Christian. She goes to her brother, not because she hesitates, but that he may share with her the burden of her irrevocable decision. Claudio's first reply is, "O heavens! it cannot be"; "Thou shalt not do't." But the very bravest of men have quailed, within the four walls of a prison

---

From Man's Unconquerable Mind (*London: Jonathan Cape Ltd.,* 1939, *reissued in* 1952), *pp.* 287–90. *Reprinted by permission of the publisher and the R. W. Chambers' Estate. This essay was first published in* Proceedings of the British Academy, XXIII (1937), *and slightly revised for the first ed. of* Man's Unconquerable Mind (1939).

[1] Matthew x, 37; Luke xiv, 26.

cell, waiting for the axe next day. I am amazed at the way critics condemn Claudio, when he breaks down, and utters his second thoughts, "Sweet sister, let me live." Isabel overwhelms him in the furious speech which we all know. And I am even more amazed at the dislike which the critics feel for the tortured Isabel. But when they assure us that their feeling towards both his creatures was shared by the gentle Shakespeare, I am then most amazed of all.

It is admitted that no greater or more moving scenes had appeared on any stage, since the masterpieces of Attic drama ceased to be acted. Yet our critics tell us that Shakespeare wrote them in a mood of "disillusionment and cynicism," "self-laceration" and, strangest of all, "weariness." [2] "A corroding atmosphere of moral suspicion" [3] hangs about this debate between "the sainted Isabella, wrapt in her selfish chastity," and "the wretched boy who in terror of death is ready to sacrifice his sister's honour." [4] Isabel's chastity, they say, is "rancid," and she is "not by any means such a saint as she looks";[5] her in-humanity is pitiless, her virtue is self-indulgent, unimaginative, and self-absorbed.[6]

And yet, think of Rose Macaulay's war-poem, "Many sisters to many brothers," and let us believe that a sister may suffer more in agony of mind than the brother can suffer in physical wounds or death. Shakespeare has made Isabel say to Claudio,

> O, were it but my life,
> I'ld throw it down for your deliverance
> As frankly as a pin.

It is standing the play on its head,[7] to say that Shakespeare wrote those words in irony and cynicism. How did he convey that to his audience? If such assumptions are allowed, we can prove anything we like, "eight years together, dinners and suppers and sleeping-hours excepted."

Isabel then, as Shakespeare sees her and asks us to see her, would frankly, joyously, give her life to save Claudio: and *"greater love hath no man than this."* And now Claudio is asking for what she

---

[2] J. DOVER WILSON, op. cit. [*The Essential Shakespeare*], pp. 116, 117.
[3] E. K. CHAMBERS, op. cit. [*Shakespeare: a Survey*], p. 214.
[4] J. DOVER WILSON, op. cit., p. 116.
[5] New Cambridge Shakespeare, *Measure for Measure*, p. xxx.
[6] U. M. ELLIS-FERMOR, op. cit. [*The Jacobean Drama*], pp. 261, 262.
[7] I borrow this very excellent phrase from W. W. Lawrence (p. 70). The brevity of a lecture compels me to pass over many points that a critic may think should have been more fully argued, but I do this the more cheerfully, because they have been already so fully discussed by Lawrence in his *Shakespeare's Problem Comedies*, 1931, and their moral emphasized in an excellent leading article in *The Times Literary Supplement* of 16 July 1931.

cannot give, and she bursts out in agony. Have the critics never seen a human soul or a human body in the extremity of torment? Physical torture Isabel thinks she could have stood without flinching. She has said so to Angelo:

> The impression of keen whips I'ld wear as rubies,
> And strip myself to death, as to a bed
> That longing have been sick for, ere I'ld yield
> My body up to shame.

To suppose that Shakespeare gave these burning words to Isabel so that we should perceive her to be selfish and cold, is to suppose that he did not know his job. The honour of her family and her religion are more to her than mere life, her own or Claudio's.

Ernest Schanzer: Isabella Reproved

This strain of legalism in Isabel has been remarked by Professor Charlton: "Too frequently she seems to regard the letter as the fundamental thing in the law," he comments.[1] And Isabel's Puritanism —which also manifests itself at times in her diction, e.g. "I have spirit to do anything that appears not foul in the truth of my spirit" (III.1.201–2)—has also not gone unnoticed. Lascelles Abercrombie, in his excellent British Academy Lecture for 1930, says of it: "When we come to Shakespeare's use of the feeling against puritanism in *Measure for Measure,* we find that the antagonist who brings into odium the popular idea of puritanism in Angelo is actually puritanism itself—the splendid and terrible puritanism of Isabella." [2]

I am not suggesting that we should do what Quiller-Couch confesses he was once almost driven to do: to examine Isabel and Angelo

---

"Isabella Reproved" (title supplied by the editor). From "Measure for Measure" by Ernest Schanzer. From The Problem Plays of Shakespeare *(New York: Schocken Books Inc., 1963; London: Routledge & Kegan Paul, Ltd., 1963), pp. 104–7. Copyright © 1963 by Ernest Schanzer. Reprinted by permission of the publishers.*

[1] *Shakespearian Comedy* (1938), p. 254.

[2] "A Plea for the Liberty of Interpreting," in *Aspects of Shakespeare* (1933), p. 236. Many years earlier Mary Suddard had written: "In Isabella and Angelo Shakespeare not only embodies two main types of Puritan, but sets forth all the advantages and defects of Puritanic training. . . . Different as its results may seem on Angelo and Isabella, the two studies point to the same conclusion: Puritanism, in its present state, unmodified, is unfit to come into contact with society. To borrow the words of Lamb, 'it is an owl that will not bear daylight' " (*op. cit.* [*Keats Shelley and Shakespeare Studies*, 1912], p. 149).

"as two pendent portraits or studies in the ugliness of Puritan hypocrisy." [3] For Isabel is no hypocrite, nor is there anything ugly about her
Puritanism. It is, as Abercrombie says, "splendid and terrible." I am
merely maintaining that throughout the play Shakespeare is showing
up certain likenesses between the two characters, that he is manipulating our feelings towards Isabel by alternately engaging and
alienating our affection for her, and that he is doing all this mainly
to make us question her decision to sacrifice her brother rather than
her virginity. He makes us question it without forcing an answer
upon us. The majority of critics have, in fact, felt that Isabel could
have acted in no other way than she did. R. W. Chambers, who must
speak for all these, declares that "whether she remains in the Convent
or no, one who is contemplating such a life can no more be expected
to sell herself into mortal sin, than a good soldier can be expected
to sell a stronghold entrusted to him." [4] (By taking it for granted that it
would be a mortal sin, Chambers begs the question. Hence the
analogy with the soldier is a false one.) There have been others—
a minority among critics, but much more numerous, I suspect, among
those mute, inglorious Bradleys that constitute the bulk of Shakespeare's readers—who have thought that Cinthio's Epitia and Whetstone's Cassandra made the more admirable choice. The manner in
which Shakespeare manipulates his material, as well as the evidence
of his other plays, suggest to me very strongly that he, too, preferred
Cassandra's choice. How he felt towards a legalistic conception of
Divine Justice is suggested by his treatment of the churlish priest in
Hamlet, who refuses Ophelia's body full burial rites because technically
her death may come under the heading of suicide:

> Her death was doubtful;
> And, but that great command o'ersways the order,
> She should in ground unsanctified have lodg'd
> Till the last trumpet; for charitable prayers,
> Shards, flints, and pebbles, should be thrown on her . . .

with Laertes' splendid reply:

> I tell thee, churlish priest,
> A minist'ring angel shall my sister be
> When thou liest howling.   (V.1. 221 ff.)

It is the kind of reply which one would like Isabel to have made
when Angelo denounces the "filthy vices" of her brother. Instead
we get her "My brother had but justice,/In that he did the thing for

---

[3] *Op. cit.* [*Measure for Measure, New Shakespeare* ed., 1922], p. xxx.
[4] *Op. cit.* [*Man's Unconquerable Mind,* 1939], p. 292.

which he died." By depicting first the inhumanity of Angelo's legalism, followed by numerous parallels between Isabel's and Angelo's characters, and then showing Isabel's legalistic view of Divine Justice, Shakespeare is, it would seem to me, strongly suggesting his own attitude towards her choice. But he leaves it sufficiently unobtrusive to allow the audience to respond to it in an uncertain, divided, or varied manner.

Measure for Measure is thus seen to conform to the definition of the Problem Play given in the Introduction. . . . We have found in it "a concern with a moral problem which is central to it, presented in such a manner that we are unsure of our moral bearings, so that uncertain and divided responses to it in the minds of the audience are possible or even probable." This view of the play is supported by Raleigh when he writes of it: "Of all Shakespeare's plays, this one comes nearest to the direct treatment of a moral problem." [5] It finds its sharpest opponent in E. E. Stoll, who declares that *Measure for Measure* is "a tragicomedy, still less than *All's Well* a problem play. No question is raised, no casuistry is engaged in, no dilemma, whether intolerable or tolerable, is put. . . . By his deviation from his source . . . Shakespeare has made the play even less of the problem kind than it had been. . . . In fact, the moral rigour in the heroine— the want of a problem—is . . . what some unsympathetic contemporary critics complain of.[6] Professor Stoll fails to see that the moral rigour of the heroine, as Shakespeare presents it, is itself at the root of the problem. That Isabel's choice does not appear to her in any way problematic—that she is shown free from all inner conflict and doubt —in no way implies that Shakespeare presents it as unproblematic and that the same freedom from conflict and doubt is experienced by the audience.

[5] *Op. cit.* [*Shakespeare,* 1907], p. 169.
[6] "*All's Well* and *Measure for Measure,*" in *From Shakespeare to Joyce* (1944), pp. 259–60.

Madeleine Doran: Two Problems in Measure for Measure

Everyone knows of the general critical dissatisfaction with the ending of *Measure for Measure.* Actually, I think Shakespeare has been at

---

"*Two Problems in* Measure for Measure" (*title supplied by the editor*). *From* "*Endeavors of Art*" *by Madeleine Doran. From* Endeavors of Art: A study of form in Elizabethan drama (*Madison: The University of Wisconsin Press, 1954*),

some pains to give it a formally satisfying ending, in the happily
ironic reversal of the "measure for measure" theme. Early in the play,
Angelo answers Isabella's plea that he temper justice with mercy,
with his announced intention to carry out justice in the strictest sense
of measure for measure. With their rôles reversed at the end of the
play, Isabella is faced with the same problem with respect to him, and
after a struggle she solves it by according him mercy. His measure
should be death, but she asks the Duke that he be given life. Angelo's
act, it is true, did not wholly overtake his bad intent, in that Isabella
was not seduced and Claudio was not executed. But Angelo had nevertheless broken the severe law of the city against fornication, the same
law for which he had held Claudio to strict account, and broken it
without Claudio's intention of marriage; moreover, he had forsworn
himself in breaking his promise to Isabella to let her brother go free.
It must be remembered, too, that Isabella did not know, at the moment she sought to excuse Angelo, that her brother was still alive.
The whole point is that she can generously find an excuse for Angelo
(though he had meant her very ill indeed), as he could not find for
Claudio, who had meant no ill at all. The eloquent words of her
plea to Angelo come back to our minds with great ironic force as he
stands to be judged at the end of the play:

> Why, all the souls that were were forfeit once;
> And He that might the vantage best have took,
> Found out the remedy. How would you be,
> If He, which is the top of judgment, should
> But judge you as you are? O! think on that,
> And mercy then will breathe within your lips,
> Like man new made.

There is another problem in the play, however, the problem of
Isabella's choice between her brother's death and the sacrifice of her
chastity; and we are troubled by the evasion of it through the device
of the substituted woman common in the *novelle*.[1] I think a careful
reading of the play shows that Shakespeare meant to put the primary
emphasis on the problem of the exercise of power, the problem he

*pp. 368–69. Copyright 1954 by the Regents of the University of Wisconsin. Re-
printed by permission of the author and publisher.*
[1] For a subtle and provocative discussion of both these problems in the play,
see Harbage, *As They Liked It*, pp. 83–84, 89–92, 126–31. Professor Harbage
observes that the ending of the play metes out exactly "measure for measure"
and is pragmatic justice, not mercy, since Angelo's evil intents have missed fire;
perhaps so, but who is it in the play who most needs forgiveness, and who
gets it? . . .

solves, and not on the problem of Isabella's chastity. Nevertheless, we cannot wholly exorcise the difficulty that is inherent in housing problems like these in what H. Harvey Wood, speaking of Marston's plays, calls "the gimcrack erections of improbable situation."

Chronology of Important Dates

	Shakespeare	The Age
1558		Accession of Queen Elizabeth I.
1564	Born at Stratford on Avon; christened April 26.	Marlowe born.
1572		Donne and Jonson born.
1582	Married to Anne Hathaway.	
1583–85	Susanna and the twins, Hamnet and Judith, born.	
1587		Kyd's *The Spanish Tragedy;* Marlowe's *Tamburlaine,* Part I.
1588–94	Performance of early comedies.	Spenser's *The Faerie Queene,* Bks. I–III (1590).
1591–92	The three *Henry VI* plays.	
1592		Marlowe's *Doctor Faustus* and *Edward II.*
1593–94	*Venus and Adonis,* and *The Rape of Lucrece* (dedicated to Earl of Southampton); *Titus Andronicus; Richard III;* Shakespeare a sharer in Lord Chamberlain's company.	Deaths of Marlowe and Kyd.
1595–96	*A Midsummer Night's Dream; Richard II; Romeo and Juliet; King John; The Merchant of Venice;* death of son, Hamnet.	Sidney's *The Defense of Poesy;* Spenser's *Amoretti and Epithalamion; The Faerie Queene,* Bks. IV–VI; *Fowre Hymnes.*

1597–98	*1* and *2 Henry IV; Much Ado about Nothing.*	Jonson's *Every Man in His Humour;* Meres' *Palladis Tamia* (Shakespeare praised as England's "most excellent" playwright).
1599–1600	*The Merry Wives of Windsor; As You Like It; Henry V; Julius Caesar; Twelfth Night;* Lord Chamberlain's Company moves to new Globe Theater.	Marston's *Antonio and Mellida* and *Antonio's Revenge;* Jonson's *Every Man Out of His Humour.*
1601–2	*Hamlet; Troilus and Cressida.*	Gaurini's *Compendio della poesia tragicomica.*
1603–4	*All's Well that Ends Well; Measure for Measure; Othello;* Lord Chamberlain's company becomes The King's Men.	(1603) Death of Elizabeth I and accession of James I; Marston's *The Malcontent.*
1605–6	*Macbeth; King Lear.*	Jonson's *Volpone* (1606).
1607–8	*Antony and Cleopatra; Timon of Athens; Coriolanus; Pericles.*	
1609–11	*Cymbeline; The Winter's Tale; The Tempest;* retirement to Stratford.	Jonson's *The Alchemist* (1610).
1616	Died at Stratford, April 23.	Jonson's *Works* published in Folio edition.
1623	First Folio edition of Shakespeare's plays.	

Notes on the Editor and Contributors

GEORGE L. GECKLE teaches Renaissance literature at the University of South Carolina. He has published articles on Shakespeare, Milton, and James Joyce and is working on the New Variorum *Measure for Measure* (ed. Mark Eccles).

ANTHONY CAPUTI is Associate Professor of English at Cornell University. He is the author of *John Marston, Satirist* and editor of *A Norton Critical Edition of Modern Drama*.

R. W. CHAMBERS (1874–1942) was Professor of English, University College, London. His publications include *Beowulf, Thomas More, "King Lear,"* and other works.

MADELEINE DORAN, Ruth C. Wallerstein Professor of English Literature at the University of Wisconsin, has written textual studies on *Henry VI, Parts II and III* and *King Lear,* has edited the two parts of Thomas Heywood's *If You Know Not Me, You Know Nobody* and Shakespeare's *A Midsummer Night's Dream,* and has several scholarly and critical essays on Elizabethan thought and Shakespearean drama.

FRANCIS FERGUSSON is Professor of Comparative Literature at Rutgers University. He is the author of *The Idea of a Theatre, Dante's Drama of the Mind: A Modern Reading of the Purgatio,* and other works.

G. WILSON KNIGHT, Emeritus Professor of English Literature at Leeds University, has been an immensely influential Shakespearean critic. His many books on Shakespeare include *The Imperial Theme, The Shakespearian Tempest, The Crown of Life,* and *The Sovereign Flower.*

MURRAY KRIEGER is Professor of English and Comparative Literature at the University of California, Irvine. His many books include *The New Apologists for Poetry, A Window to Criticism: Shakespeare's "Sonnets" and Modern Poetics,* and *The Play and Place of Criticism.*

WILLIAM WITHERLE LAWRENCE (1876–1958) taught for many years at Columbia University and was the author of several works, including *Medieval Story, Beowulf and Epic Tradition,* and *Chaucer and the Canterbury Tales.*

J. W. LEVER, Lecturer in English at the University of Durham, has written *The Elizabethan Love Sonnet* and other works.

KENNETH MUIR, King Alfred Professor of English Literature at the University of Liverpool, has edited *Shakespeare: The Comedies* for Prentice-Hall's Twentieth Century Views series and both *King Lear* and *Macbeth* for the Arden Shakespeare. He has also written several other books on Shakespeare, Milton, Sidney, and Wyatt.

ELIZABETH MARIE POPE, Associate Professor of English at Mills College, is the author of *Paradise Regained: The Tradition and the Poem* and other works.

ERNEST SCHANZER, who teaches English Literature at the University of Munich, is editor of *Shakespeare's Appian* and has written other works.

E. M. W. TILLYARD (1889–1962) was Master of Jesus College, Cambridge, and is well-known for his many books on Shakespeare and Milton and such studies as *The English Epic and Its Background* and *The Elizabethan World Picture*.

Selected Bibliography

Bennett, Josephine Waters. *Measure for Measure as Royal Entertainment.* New York and London: Columbia University Press, 1966. A recent study that focusses on the influence of James I on *Measure for Measure.*

Bradbrook, M. C. "Authority, Truth and Justice in *Measure for Measure,*" *Review of English Studies,* XVII (1941), 385–99. A good essay on the Morality-play background of *Measure for Measure.*

Dickinson, John W. "Renaissance Equity and *Measure for Measure,*" *Shakespeare Quarterly,* XIII (1962), 287–97. Ascending triad of values in *Measure for Measure* involves law, equity, and Christian mercy; "equity is invoked principally through . . . Escalus."

Dodds, W. M. T. "The Character of Angelo in Measure for Measure," *Modern Language Review,* XLI (1946), 246–55. A good analysis of a complex character whose situation "is, as it were, a diagram of a tragedy."

Lascelles, Mary. *Shakespeare's "Measure for Measure."* London: The Athlone Press of the University of London, 1953. An excellent and thoroughgoing discussion that includes analysis of every scene in the play.

Lawrence, William W. "*Measure for Measure* and Lucio," *Shakespeare Quarterly,* IX (1958), 443–53. A good general discussion of the play and of Lucio's function in particular.

Leech, Clifford. "The 'Meaning' of *Measure for Measure,*" *Shakespeare Survey,* III (1950), 66–73. A rather literal-minded argument against a simplified view of the play as a representation of Christian doctrine.

Rossiter, A. P. "The Problem Plays" and "Measure for Measure," two chapters in *Angel with Horns and Other Shakespeare Lectures,* ed. Graham Storey. London: Longmans, Green & Co., Ltd., 1961; New York: Theatre Arts Books, 1961, pp. 108–28, 152–70. Contains a good discussion of the tragicomic vision in *Measure for Measure.*

Stevenson, David Lloyd. *The Achievement of Shakespeare's "Measure for Measure."* Ithaca, N.Y.: Cornell University Press, 1966. A sensitive reading of the play, but with an antihistorical bias.

Traversi, D. A. "Measure for Measure," *Scrutiny,* XI (1942), 40–58. Reprinted with slight revisions in Traversi's *An Approach to Shakespeare,* 2nd ed. Garden City, N.Y.: Doubleday & Co., Inc., 1956, pp. 107–25. Perceptive criticism of the play's diction and imagery.

Wilson, Harold S. "Action and Symbol in *Measure for Measure* and *The Tempest,*" *Shakespeare Quarterly,* IV (1953), 375–84. An interesting comparison of the dukes in *Measure for Measure* and *The Tempest* who effect "the moral order of things as divinely authorized."

TWENTIETH CENTURY
INTERPRETATIONS

MAYNARD MACK, *Series Editor*
Yale University

NOW AVAILABLE
Collections of Critical Essays
ON

ADVENTURES OF HUCKLEBERRY FINN
ALL FOR LOVE
THE AMBASSADORS
ARROWSMITH
AS YOU LIKE IT
BLEAK HOUSE
THE BOOK OF JOB
THE CASTLE
DOCTOR FAUSTUS
DON JUAN
DUBLINERS
THE DUCHESS OF MALFI
ENDGAME
EURIPIDES' ALCESTIS
THE FALL OF THE HOUSE OF USHER
THE FROGS
GRAY'S ELEGY
THE GREAT GATSBY
GULLIVER'S TRAVELS
HAMLET
HARD TIMES

(continued on next page)

(continued from previous page)